Acknowledgments

No industry changes faster than the computer industry, with its rapid technological innovations. We are grateful for the revisions that Kevin Crider has made to Chapter 11. His contribution to the book is greatly appreciated.

D1397611

CHAPTER ONE

Endless Career Opportunities

Computers are simply everywhere—offices, zoos, outer space, planes, trains, automobiles, grocery stores, furniture stores, schools, hospitals, farms, banks, libraries, movie studios, radio stations, Internet cafés, and homes. It's almost impossible to spend a day without seeing a computer. The computerization of the entire world is no longer a dream; it is fast becoming a reality. By the year 2007, it is estimated that there will be more than one billion personal computers (PCs) worldwide. Most are in the United States, followed by Japan, China, Germany, the United Kingdom, and France. PC usage is also growing rapidly in many large countries, such as India, Brazil, and Russia. Believe it or not, according to Dr. Egil Juliussen of the Computer Industry Almanac, more people in the United States in 2005 actually used computers than cell phones. And this will remain true for several more years.

The computer industry is fast moving and exciting, and it is rapidly changing the way we do business and handle so many activities, from listening to music to playing games. Less than fifty years ago, most computers were enormous, exotic machines so big they filled a room and were only found at a few large companies. Even the largest supercomputers today have shrunk in size. And we certainly know how laptops are becoming smaller and smaller. Today, there are almost as many computers in the United States as there are people. And personal computers are now more powerful than the supercomputers of the past. Nowhere has the computer affected our lives more than with the advent of the Internet, which has truly changed how we communicate with each other.

Many visionary and colorful people have played important roles in the developing computer industry. Most are young, and many are millionaires—a few are billionaires. Computer buffs are well aware of Steve Jobs and Steve Wozniak, who created the Apple computer in a garage, and of Bill Gates and Paul Allen, who founded Microsoft while Bill was still in his teens. Then there is David Filo, who doesn't wear shoes and sleeps on the carpet in his cramped office with his head jammed under his desk about once a week. He and Jerry Yang founded Yahoo, one of the two most popular Internet search engines, while they were graduate students at Stanford University. Yahoo began as an idea, grew into a hobby, and then turned into a wildly successful company. The latest young geniuses are Larry Page and Sergey Brin, who are only in their early thirties. They are the founders of the Google Internet search engine through which two hundred million searches are made each day. At their company headquarters in Silicon Valley, certain quirks such as roller-hockey games in the parking lot and an on-site masseuse keep the staff happy. Perhaps you might one day have the insight to join these computer-industry pioneers in creating a company based on a revolutionary new idea.

The Birth and Growth of the Computer

Before you begin to explore the intriguing careers available to you today in the computer industry, you need to become acquainted with its history and its pioneers. Looking at the past to recognize trends can help you predict some elements of the future.

The computer's parents were the mathematicians and scientists who desired a machine that would reduce the time required to do complex mathematical calculations. Their efforts resulted first in the invention of the abacus approximately five thousand years ago. Ancient Babylonians, Egyptians, Chinese, Greeks, and Romans all used devices with movable counters to improve the speed and accuracy of their calculations. It was not until the 1600s, however, that the first mechanical calculating machines were built. One of the more notable machines was built in 1642 by Blaise Pascal, a French mathematician and scientist, to help handle his father's business accounts. Pascal's machine used rotating wheels with teeth to add and subtract numbers of up to eight digits. The name *Pascal* is remembered today by computer buffs every time they use the computer language that bears his name. Just a few years later, in 1673, Gottfried Leibniz developed a more complex calculating device that also had the capability of multiplying, dividing, and finding square roots.

The Father of the Computer

Early calculating machines were not reliable, and all had problems carrying over numbers in addition. Mathematicians, scientists, engineers, navigators, and others who needed to do more than very simple calculations were forced to rely on printed mathematical tables that were riddled with errors. Disconcerted by the enormous effort required to make calculation tables, Charles Babbage, an English mathematician, developed the idea of an automatic calculating device called the difference engine. Financial and technical difficulties precluded the building of the complete machine; however, the section of the machine that was completed is regarded as the first automatic calculator. Nevertheless, Babbage is not primarily remembered for the difference engine but for his design of a machine that he called the analytical engine. This machine, which was designed to perform complicated calculations, contained the basic elements of modern electronic computers. Babbage's machine separated memory and storage and was programmable. Babbage kept developing and refining the design of this machine until his death, but the problems that had beset him in attempting to build the difference engine discouraged him from making a concerted effort to build the analytical engine.

Interest waned in the development of automatic calculation machines after Babbage's death. Progress was made, however, in developing calculators. By the end of the 1800s, reliable calculating machines were readily available. In addition, data processing became automated through Herman Hollerith's development of an automatic punch-card tabulating machine. He had been commissioned by the United States Census Bureau to resolve the crisis the bureau faced in handling the 1890 census data. Millions of immigrants had turned the process of analyzing the 1880 census data into an almost eight-year task. With the nation growing so rapidly, the Census Bureau feared that the 1890 census data would never be analyzed before the next census was taken. Herman Hollerith's data processing device saved the day, permitting the data to be analyzed in just two and one-half years. Hollerith had developed a code that used a pattern of punched holes to represent data. His machine recognized whether or not a hole was covered, and electricity passed through the holes to activate motors that moved counters, which gave out totals. Number-crunching industries such as accounting, banking, and insurance enthusiastically embraced the use of perforated cards to handle data. In fact, punched-card equipment was used in data processing until the late 1950s. Even today some elements of Hollerith's code still are being used in computers to read input and format output. The Tabulating Machine Company that Hollerith organized to sell equipment for commercial use went on to become one of the companies that merged to form IBM in 1911.

The Modern Computer Age Begins

After Hollerith constructed his tabulating machine, several computing devices were developed. These computers were never well publicized. ENIAC (Electronic Numerical Integrator Analyzer and Computer), however, gained instant worldwide attention when it was introduced at a press conference in 1946. ENIAC was a gigantic machine—over one hundred feet long and eight feet deep and weighing eighty tons—developed by J. Presper Eckert and John W.

Mauchly, two engineers at the University of Pennsylvania. ENIAC, the first fully electronic digital computer, worked approximately one thousand times faster than previous machines. It could perform five thousand arithmetic operations in a second. ENIAC proved that large electronic systems were technically possible. Unfortunately, ENIAC had a serious flaw. It was very time consuming to program because switches had to be set and boards had to be wired by hand. It took days to set up programs that took only seconds to run. In spite of its flaws, ENIAC inaugurated the modern computer age.

John von Neumann solved ENIAC's flaws by introducing the idea that programs could be coded as numbers and stored with data in a computer's memory. His idea was used in building EDVAC (Electronic Discrete Variable Automatic Computer), which was the first stored-program digital computer.

By 1945, the Census Bureau was again drowning in a sea of paper. Eckert and Mauchly signed a contract to develop a new computer to solve the bureau's problems. They also contracted to build computers for three other clients: Northrop Aircraft Corporation, Prudential Life Insurance, and the A. C. Nielsen Company. Eckert and Mauchly developed a more advanced electronic digital computer for their customers, which they called UNIVAC I (Universal Automatic Computer). Unfortunately, their financial skills did not match their computer expertise, and they were forced to sell the company to Remington Rand in 1950. UNIVAC achieved fame in 1952 when it was introduced to television to predict the results of the presidential election. UNIVAC predicted that Eisenhower would win in a landslide, but the people at CBS did not agree with the prediction. The next day everyone learned that the computer had been correct and the humans incorrect.

Remington Rand's success with UNIVAC inspired Thomas Watson Jr. to have IBM enter the fledgling computer business. Within a few years, IBM secured a dominant position in the industry with its moderately priced computers, which tied easily into existing punch-card installations.

The Inventions That Revolutionized Computers

ENIAC and UNIVAC I used vacuum tubes for arithmetic and memory-switching functions. These tubes were very expensive, used considerable power, and gave off an enormous amount of heat. In 1948, the transistor was invented at Bell Telephone Laboratories, spelling the end of the vacuum tube. By using this new technology, second-generation computers became much smaller than earlier computers, had increased storage capacity, and were able to process data much faster.

The invention of the integrated circuit in 1958 by Jack Kilby of Texas Instruments signaled the start of another new era in computing. Previously, individual components had to be wired together; now it was possible to print the wiring and the components together on silicon circuit chips. By 1974, continuous technological progress through large-scale integration (LSI) made it possible to pack thousands of transistors and related electronic elements on a single chip, and the PC revolution began. From 1965 until recently, the number of components per integrated circuit doubled about every year. This trend has now slowed to doubling every eighteen months and is gradually moving to doubling every two years as it is getting harder to develop new technology so quickly. Nevertheless, with each technological advance, computers continue to become faster, cheaper, and smaller. Furthermore, as integrated circuits permitted the design of computers with ever more memory capacity, the need for reliable programs generated the birth of the software industry.

The Age of Personal Computers

Spurred on by the development of video games, the 1970s saw computer companies introduce personal computers. The 1980s saw intense competition in a very crowded PC field. Since then, companies have disappeared and been absorbed by other companies. Today's major players are IBM, Hewlett-Packard, Sony, Hitachi, Fujitsu, Dell, Apple, and Gateway. The desire to have computers always at our fingertips has led to the recent popularity of laptops. These ever-smaller computers are now capturing 35 percent of the PC market share.

While we tend to think of PCs when we hear the word *computer*, supercomputers have emerged that are able to do tasks that would take thousands of years for a PC to complete. These supercomputers are simulating weather systems, earthquakes, and chemical reactions in molecules. In 2005, IBM's giant computer at the Lawrence Livermore National Laboratory was the world's fastest. It could handle 136.8 calculations per second, and IBM plans to double the size of this system by 2006.

A Quick Look at Computer Buffs

Everyone today needs to be computer literate to some extent in order to survive. Computer buffs, however, are a special breed. They try to spend as much of their waking time as they can working, playing games, or simply enjoying such activities as listening to music or viewing movies on their computers. They no longer have to leave their computers to go shopping because nearly everything imaginable can be purchased online. The magnetic pull of the computer dictates most of what computer buffs do. Today, much of their time is spent online surfing the Net or chatting with other computer buffs. Most have forsaken pen and paper correspondence for e-mail. When computer buffs are away from their computers, they spend hours browsing through computer stores, studying computer magazines, and reading about computers. Contemplating how they can upgrade their computers is another favored pastime, as is devising new programs to meet their needs. The computer truly invades virtually every aspect of a computer buff's everyday life. You will even find confirmed computer buffs playing solitaire on their computers.

Computer buffs do not have to limit their interest in computers to the role of a hobby. They can readily find satisfying careers that let them spend their working hours in jobs devoted entirely to the computer. The computer revolution is here, and new and exciting jobs in the industry are emerging at an astonishing speed. Today there is scarcely a business or industry that does not utilize the computer in some way. From agriculture to aerospace, there are many exciting careers for computer buffs. The computer was *Time* magazine's Man of the Year in 1982. Working with a computer will be the job of the twenty-first century, and computer buffs will be our heroes because they are creating and using technology to make positive things happen.

An Overview of Today's Careers for Computer Buffs

This book is dedicated to helping all computer buffs realize their dreams of finding jobs that allow them to work with computers on company time. Here is a bird's-eye view of some of the careers you will read about in this book.

Hardware Careers

People with vision are employed to create computers—from laptops to supercomputers—as well as the peripheral devices essential to their operation. They need college degrees in computer science or electrical engineering. Jobs are not limited to research and development, as computers also need to be manufactured, sold, and serviced. Most jobs are with the makers of computer components.

Software Careers

Without software, the computer is just a box. It is software that tells a computer what to do. Developing software is very labor intensive. Programmers are needed to write the system software every computer requires to manage its operation. Programmers also create the programs that tell the computer how to perform specific tasks, from word processing to surfing the Net. Besides developing software programs, computer buffs are needed to sell the programs and provide documentation and training for program users.

Computer Services Careers

As the number of computers in the world approaches a billion units, more and more people are needed to provide a variety of services to computer users. A growing employment area exists for those who can plan, design, and implement computer systems and networks. Furthermore, with so many companies drowning in paperwork, transaction-processing services need employees to process all kinds of transactions, from payroll to medical records. The current explosion of information also has led to the creation of information service providers who use computers to collect, manipulate, and disseminate information (usually over the Internet) about all kinds of topics, from stock market quotations to statistics on school enrollment. Then, to keep all the data stored on computers safe, there are companies offering off-site backup services.

Systems Analyst Careers

Systems analysts do not just bury their noses in computers. They are professional problem solvers who listen to computer users in order to meet their needs and solve their problems. Systems analysts improve existing systems and may even design new systems. All of their work is designed to give users the computer resources they need. These analysts are the "people persons" in the computer profession, and they are among the most sought-after employees in the industry.

Computer Operations Careers

Computer systems must be kept running, whether they are operated by airlines, catalog stores, or the Internal Revenue Service. For many organizations this means round-the-clock jobs for computer systems operators. The computers and all their related machines must operate smoothly. When systems are down, the operations staff must get them online again as quickly as possible. Running the computer also involves entering data and instructions into the computer and handling the computer's output.

Information Systems Careers

Computers no longer are used just to handle everyday business tasks such as billing and payroll. Now computers provide all types of information to help management make decisions about products, sales, marketing, and almost every aspect of a company's business.

Computers have the capacity to spew out so much information that managers are now required to manage databases of stored corporate information and determine what new material should be developed. Besides handling these new tasks, managers of information systems purchase equipment and software and supervise all the other data processing tasks.

Computer Careers in Special Areas

Computer buffs can use the computer to express their creativity, whether it is in design, manufacturing, animation, music, or entertainment. One of the fastest-growing areas of computer use is computer-aided design (CAD). These are the jobs that let computer buffs design and plan automobiles, houses, clothing, and such computer staples as microchips and integrated circuits. Computer-aided manufacturing (CAM) lets people be involved with the fabrication of products under computer control.

If you have an artistic flair, you can find jobs that combine this talent with your interest in the computer. For example, in the music arena, you can use the computer to create compositions and play a variety of instruments.

Visual artists can use the amazing graphics capacity of computers to create commercial artwork and all types of special effects seen in TV shows and movies. Jobs in animation have changed dramatically with increasing use of the computer.

Internet Careers

The Internet has made a profound impact on our personal lives as well as on how companies do business. In just a few short years, it has become the norm for businesses to have websites and do some of their business online. Plus, there are now many businesses, such as the gigantic Amazon.com, that deal only with online customers. Businesses need savvy technical types who can help them get online, who can develop software for the Net, and who have the skills to be Webmasters or Web designers. People who can advertise, market, and sell products and services on the Internet are also in demand. In addition, hardware and software companies design products that make it easier to use the computer in our personal lives and to do business online. They are looking for innovative computer buffs to help them in this continuing task. And there are always opportunities for entrepreneurial people to build their own Internet businesses.

Computer Careers in Jobs from A to Z

Banks, insurance companies, retailers, hospitals, and manufacturers all have computers playing essential roles in the operation of their businesses. Airlines, supermarkets, and newspapers depend heavily on computers. No matter what occupation you choose, from A to Z, whether it is an airline pilot, a doctor, a librarian, or a zookeeper, you will most likely find yourself using the computer in your job.

Computer Careers in the Future

The range of job options for computer buffs continues to widen as more and more new ways are discovered to use the computer. Completely new jobs will emerge as computers become even more skilled at making decisions, more capable of reading handwriting and understanding the human voice, and better able to communicate with other computers—in short, "smarter." More careers are emerging in entertainment as Hollywood and the computer become more closely linked. At the same time, emerging technology will change the nature of many jobs, and some of today's jobs will disappear.

A Computer Buff's Dream—Finding a Career with the Machine

The inventors of the first computers had no idea of the numerous ways computers would be used. Nor did they ever realize how many jobs would be created by this fairly young industry. The Federal Bureau of Labor Statistics reports that computer jobs will be one of the top two job-growth fields in the early years of the twenty-first century. Nevertheless, computer jobs have lost some luster for young technical types. Tens of thousands of engineering and manufacturing jobs have moved to developing countries, making the job search more competitive. Many new jobs in the computer field are with companies seeking applicants who not only have technical expertise but also business skills.

The Job Search

Until recently, job searches typically have been conducted by reading want ads and contacting companies by mail or phone. There is a new element now in job searching. It is the Internet with its huge databases of job listings. Plus, it is now possible to go online to chat with career counselors, practice your interview skills, and go to a website to learn more about a company and see what job opportunities may be available—all without leaving the home computer. The Internet has the advantage of letting you search for jobs whenever you want. Computer buffs, however, need to be reminded not to abandon traditional job-hunting resources. It's still important to look at ads in newspapers and journals, contact companies about possible jobs, network, and have both a print and online resume. Furthermore, don't expect to get a job just by sending out your resume online. Only about 10 percent of all jobs are secured in this way.

One of the very best resources on the Internet for learning about employment opportunities and job resources is *The Riley Guide* (www.rileyguide.com). It will tell you how to incorporate the Internet in your job search, find Net career planning services, prepare your resume for the Net, and find the best research sources for your job search. It will also tell you how to find salary information. An excellent print resource is *The Guide to Internet Job Searching* by Margaret Riley Dikel and Frances E. Roehm.

Just a glance at the following listings from the Internet will give you an idea of what an excellent resource it is for discovering job opportunities:

ASSOCIATE WEB DEVELOPER

Responsibilities: Building and maintaining HTML Web pages and ensuring our pages meet the highest standard of technical quality.

Qualifications: Experience building and managing a commercial website, comprehensive technical understanding of HTML and the Internet; knowledge of JAVA, ActiveX, and CGI scripting a plus.

TECHNICAL SUPPORT REPRESENTATIVE

The primary duty is to assist customers via the telephone and e-mail with connectivity problems. We also provide first-level support for the use of various Internet-related products contained on our Web page.

Typical duties and responsibilities:

- provide excellent customer service
- assist in resolving technical issues via phone and e-mail
- provide a high level of professional and competent support to all customers

- ensure that individual and department goals of problem resolution and call duration are met
- act in a mature and professional manner toward customers, vendors, and other company employees at all times

Required abilities:

- flexibility to work staggered hours
- excellent customer-service skills
- strong aptitude for problem solving
- previous Internet experience desired
- experience that demonstrates the ability to effectively communicate with customers over the phone
- experience with computers and operating systems

Hours: All shifts; training to be done during normal business hours. Part- and full-time positions available.

JUNIOR PROGRAMMER IN THE TECHNOLOGY DEPARTMENT

Education requirement: Bachelor's degree in computer science or other relevant area of study

Professional experience: All experience levels

Job description: Entry-level programmer to work as part of a small development team tasked with the design, development, and support of an internal, Web-based application. Support and maintenance of existing systems also required.

Required skills:

- ability to take direction and suggestions from superiors and coworkers and follow through to completion

- must work well in a team environment
- capable of learning in a fast-paced environment
- strong problem-solving skills
- good communication skills

ORDER-ENTRY CLERK

You will be responsible for coordinating, reviewing, and inputting advertising insertion orders into a database. The job requires a high school diploma, or equivalent, and two or more years of order-input experience. You must have excellent data-entry skills and proficiency with Excel. Requires good organizational and phone skills and ability to follow through with pending issues. General database experience required, preferably with Microsoft Access.

Job Qualifications

Computer buffs seem to be welded to their machines. The unbreakable bonds they forge with their computers may lead them to gain such expertise that no special training will be required for them to begin their careers in the computer industry. Computer buffs with the appropriate know-how may be employed with little training as computer service technicians, salespeople, telecommunications technicians, and computer operators. Today, more and more applicants for professional-level jobs in the computer industry have college degrees. Some computer buffs have been extremely successful without completing college (Bill Gates of Microsoft Corporation and Steven Jobs of Apple). Nevertheless, as the computer industry matures, more and more firms are requiring successful applicants for professional-level positions to have college degrees. Although majors in computer science did not exist forty years ago, companies are increasingly expecting those who are interested in the technical or systems side of computers to have this degree from a quality program. Since computers are used in so many different arenas, job applicants have an advantage if they combine computer study with another area, such as engineering, mathematics, logic, economics, business, science, art, or music.

As is true in most occupations today, successful applicants for computer positions will have logged many hours in part-time jobs, in internships, or in cooperative education programs in the computer field before applying for full-time positions.

Where the Jobs Are

In the 1990s, Silicon Valley had the reputation for being the center of the computer world. If you were interested in a career in the computer industry then, the valley would have been your career destination. Much of today's valuable computer technology is still being created in Silicon Valley.

However, outsourcing is sending thousands of once-desirable computer jobs overseas. Plus, there was a period in the early 2000s when investment in new computer companies fell off and a large number of layoffs occurred. Today, investment in new companies is again accelerating, brightening the job picture in Silicon Valley.

Other states that have a large number of computer companies creating both hardware and software are Massachusetts, Illinois, New York, and Texas. And, of course, Washington is the home of Microsoft.

It is very important to understand that computer jobs are no longer limited to computer companies. There are many opportunities with every organization that uses computer technology, from the government to the smallest firms.

Learning Even More About Computer Careers

Computer buffs know that the computer industry is changing so rapidly that books can be outdated even before they make it to the library shelf. Being aware of what is going on in the computer industry is absolutely essential for finding the perfect job. Going online as well as reading current issues of such computer periodicals as *PC Magazine*, *PC World*, and *MacWorld* are the best ways to keep abreast of what is happening in the world of computers. You also can learn more about careers and the computer industry by contacting the many professional organizations associated with the industry.

CHAPTER TWO

Hardware Careers

I n homes, libraries, Internet cafés, offices, parks, airplanes, and just about everywhere, people can be seen working on their personal computers. These small, single-user computers are everywhere. Computers, however, range in size and power from small, wearable computers integrated into watches and cell phones to the huge, extremely fast supercomputers performing hundreds of millions of calculations per second. Each and every one of these computers is a programmable electronic device that can store, retrieve, and process data. They are composed of software programs that make the computers work; peripheral devices that are used to input, output, and store data; and the computer processor, which is the actual computer in charge of everything that happens. All of the computer chips, circuit boards, and peripheral devices (keyboards, mice, joysticks, monitors, printers, speakers, disks, tapes, and communication devices) are referred to as hardware. If you can see it, it's hardware.

Working with Computers and Peripheral Equipment

The individuals who are actively involved in the design and building of hardware are usually computer or electrical engineers. Of course, assemblers, inspectors, technicians, production staff, product managers, quality-control experts, sales and marketing people, education specialists, technical writers, and maintenance people also play key roles in bringing computers to individuals and organizations.

If you want to work with hardware, you would typically be employed at a computer or computer component manufacturer or vendor, from Hewlett-Packard to Apple to Dell to thousands of other companies. You may be involved with computers, parts used in computers, or peripherals. No longer are jobs concentrated at computer manufacturers; now it is highly possible that you would work at a company that manufactures chips, disk drives, or other components that can be used with different computers. You may find a job within a large, well-established company, such as Intel, Sony, or IBM, or with a new company.

If you are seriously thinking about a career in the computer industry, you must keep track of current trends to make solid career decisions. Furthermore, competition is so fierce in the computer industry that giant firms can stumble and newcomers can rapidly appear and disappear.

Computer Engineering

Whenever you see a finished computer product, whether it is a personal computer or a printer, an engineer had to play a big role in its creation. These engineers, who frequently work in teams, must have considerable technical prowess to design, develop, test, and oversee the manufacture of computers and peripheral equipment. A minimum of a bachelor's degree in electrical or computer engineering is essential, and graduate course work is often needed. Many engineers hold advanced degrees in complementary fields. Thus an engineer with a bachelor's degree in electrical engineering might have a master's degree in computer engineering. At the same time, engineers wanting to hold managerial positions may get advanced degrees in business. Because technological advances come so rapidly in the computer field, continuous study is necessary to keep skills up-to-date. Continuing education courses are offered by employers, hardware vendors, colleges, and private training institutions.

To advance in their careers, engineers who prefer hands-on experience can choose to stay on the technical side, climbing the career path from junior engineer to such positions as senior engineer, engineer, principle engineer, or project leader. Others can elect to become managers or supervisors, roles in which most of their time is devoted to managerial responsibilities and only a limited time is spent on engineering.

A Look at Salaries

The number of computer hardware engineers is not large (fewer than eighty thousand) when compared to the many more who work with software or computer applications. Entry-level salaries in computer engineering depend greatly upon the degree held. Individuals with bachelor's degrees can expect to receive a beginning salary of more than $50,000 per year, while those with master's degrees average closer to $65,000. The average income of computer hardware engineers is more than $72,000. However, the top 10 percent in this field earn more than $100,000.

Developing a Microprocessor

A microprocessor is an integrated circuit on a silicon chip. Equip it with primary and secondary storage and input and output devices and you have a microcomputer. Much of the engineering work in hardware design occurs at the chip level. Just out of college in the early nineties with a degree in electrical engineering, Curtis Shrote wanted to design chips. Those positions, however, were filled on the microprocessor team he joined at Motorola. Nevertheless, Curtis chose this job because he liked the idea of being on a team assigned to develop a general-purpose microprocessor that had 1.3 million devices on it and would run the software for an operating system. The microprocessor was being designed for the workstation market and would go into a computer the size of a pizza box.

When Curtis first went to Motorola, the design team had already talked to customers and determined what they wanted on the chip. The original team ranged from fifty to one hundred members, mostly electrical engineers. The project was headed by three first-line managers who dealt with the team members on a daily basis. One was a senior design engineer whose job was to see that everything was done correctly and to oversee the junior engineers and less-experienced engineers like Curtis. There were also subteams, and Curtis was assigned to the cache team. (A cache is a storage area that keeps frequently accessed data or program instructions readily available in memory on the chip.) His subteam of five core people—which consisted of three engineers with master's degrees, one with a bachelor's degree and prior design experience, and Curtis—clearly represented the level of expertise hardware engineers must have.

This subteam was responsible for logic design, data cache control, and instruction cache control. Curtis was given the responsibility of functional verification (locating and correcting errors) on the cache control unit on the chip. This involved designing an external simulation environment and writing test cases for all cache areas on the chip. Once the chip was in real silicon, he checked in actual tests what could not be simulated earlier.

Projects at Motorola typically take from six months to four years to complete. Curtis's project took four years. Toward the end of the project, his subteam was downsized, and Curtis started doing some design work as he corrected errors. Curtis also started working on a new project, which was to produce multiple products for the M-Core microprocessor architecture. He became the team manager of a group responsible for design verification systems. This did not involve hardware design but the development of automated test-case generation software tools written in C++, simulation reference models, utilization of formal verification tools, and advanced system models written in Verilog used for verification.

Career Path. Once he gained more experience, Curtis began to advance along the career path toward being a senior engineer, a position that requires considerable work experience. He followed both technical and managerial paths, and during that project, Curtis completed his master's degree in computer engineering, a move that Motorola strongly supported. After three years, he earned his degree from National Technological University by taking Accreditation Board for Engineering and Technology (ABET) courses on site and on company time. The courses were live or pretaped presentations of courses approved by ABET that had been taught and recorded at ABET schools. Curtis was able to phone and talk to the instructors of these courses. It is quite important for individuals wishing to have a solid background in hardware engineering to be graduates of a school with an accredited computer science or engineering program. You can see a list of these schools at www.abet.org.

During the late nineties, Curtis decided that he needed more flexibility in experience within the traditional computer science industry. He found an intriguing position as a research engineer within one of the research divisions at the University of Texas in the specialty area of computer security. Within that position he learned network security, data mining, and machine learning techniques as well as computer administration. The objectivity and skills that he had developed within his former verification role greatly facilitated his ability to understand computer security threats and develop prototype systems to deal with detecting them. He was part of a team that developed prototype software systems utilizing databases, data mining, and machine learning techniques to detect computer intrusions and alert computer security monitoring personnel. Research was conducted in a number of areas for clients contracting directly with his team.

Now Curtis has returned to Motorola once again in a verification role as a member of an experienced test improvement team focused on quality and instilling better processes supporting verification. However, he is no longer supporting silicon design. He is now within the Mobile Devices Business focused on cell-phone development. His prior experience has enhanced his ability to function in this new environment. He has skills to analyze and identify security concerns, leverage databases, understand hardware issues, and develop new tools in support of the development of consumer products that people use every day.

Education. As a child Curtis was thoroughly intrigued by the computers at his father's workplace. Furthermore, his father, an information systems manager, would talk to his family all the time about the business side of computers. By junior high, Curtis had decided that he wanted a career in the computer industry. After investigating a number of schools, Curtis elected to attend Purdue University and obtain a dual degree in electrical and computer engineering. Although initially he was not interested in taking part in the school's cooperative education (co-op) program, interviews with companies participating in the program made him change his mind. Co-op programs let students alternate studying at college with an off-campus job. Students are able to earn all or a great part of the cost of college. The Purdue program required five semesters of work to obtain a cooperative education certificate. Curtis worked off campus in the computer industry for six semesters.

Students must interview with companies and be selected to participate in the co-op program. Curtis had several choices, and he decided on a program at the IBM facility in Kingston, New York. There he was assigned to work in facilities engineering, updating building floor plans. Although Curtis had his heart set on working in chip design, he knew it was not realistic to get such a position for a first assignment. Nevertheless, he was quite pleased to be working for a major computer firm, as co-op experiences often lead to job offers in the future. Like all co-op students, Curtis had to interview for each subsequent off-campus job. Since IBM lets you change departments, he moved to the interconnect products group after his first co-op experience and stayed with this department, working on a variety of projects for the rest of his time off campus. The department built network boxes that interconnect mainframes and connect mainframes with peripherals. Although he wasn't doing design work, he had the advantage of working with an actual design, saw a long-term project evolve from simulation to actual system integration, and observed the turnover in management and employees. Curtis believes that working at IBM in the cooperative education program gave him a better idea of the courses he needed at school plus the obvious benefit of experience in the computer industry. In the semester before graduation, Curtis interviewed with five companies and was offered a job by every one.

Working in Research and Development

A job in research and development is the dream of many computer buffs who are eager to be involved in the front end of developing a product. For Loyal Mealer, this dream became a reality when he started his career as an engineer in research and development in the Scientific Instruments Division at Hewlett-Packard. He was able to dive immediately into working on the design of an analog/digital board for a research-grade mass spectrometer— work that was done using a drafting board, mechanical pencil, and electric eraser.

Loyal was able to design immediately because of his years as a computer buff and his work experience and because many schools are now giving their students hands-on design experience. He holds a bachelor's degree in electrical engineering/computer science. Without design experience in college, he would have needed a master's degree to handle this job.

Career Path. After one year, Loyal became a hardware design engineer. For the next few years, he designed many circuit boards and was even the sole designer for one set of a dozen circuit boards, which was fun and immensely satisfying work. Loyal became a hardware technical lead designer and then a project manager, where he led a small team while also doing the hardware design for an array processor board. Twelve years after starting with Hewlett-Packard, he became a section manager for research-grade mass spectrometers in the research and development department. In this position, he directly managed ten engineers and two project managers. This involved evaluating their work and managing their career paths. He also managed some projects directly. Although he sometimes offered engineers design help, Loyal says that the higher you climb in management, the harder it is to keep up with technology. For individuals in this position, the next career step is into a research and development lab manager position or some type of marketing or manufacturing management position. He moved into a position in manufacturing (manufacturing engineering manager), where he managed forty engineers and technical specialists.

After several years in that position, Loyal decided to broaden his experience at Hewlett-Packard and took a position managing a software application engineering team in a large information technology (IT) group on the computer side of the business. This was a completely different experience as he had moved out of hardware design and into software services. In this position, he was able to work with employees from many business units and to learn how the company's products and services met their needs. Loyal's team was involved in streamlining processes to reduce costs as well as introducing new collaboration services such as improved messaging (e-mail) and shared online teamwork spaces. As the company evolved, Loyal decided to take a break from management and accept a position as a senior technology strategist, where he works today investigating future technologies and helping to plan services the company provides to its customers. For this job, he has found it immensely valuable to have had many years of experience in different departments in the company. It has given him a deep appreciation for how products are developed and how things get done in a large corporation.

Advice. The technology industry has undergone tremendous change over the past half-dozen years. With the economic downturn in this country and the increasing trend toward off-shoring higher-level technical jobs, demand for entry-level engineers is not as strong as in the past. There is, however, still a need for experienced technology specialists.

Loyal's advice for students interested in working in the technology field is to get a technical bachelor's degree (electrical engineering or computer science) to provide a broad engineering foundation and then to get a master's degree with a specialty in an area of particular need at the time (information management, data mining, business intelligence, and so on). It is also important to find internships or part-time jobs while going to school to add a practical component to one's resume.

Engineering Microchip Applications

The design of any complex machine or system—be it an automobile or a microchip—is always broken down into several specialized areas. For an automobile, there are designers in charge of designing engines, transmissions, radiators, and safety door locks. For a microchip, there are physicists who know how to implant the right kind of impurity to make the silicon the right kind of semiconductor and to interconnect circuits with the right kind of metal. There are also circuit designers who know how to pack transistors as tightly as possible, and there are logic designers who can implement any desired logic function at the highest speed using the smallest possible number of components.

Designers start with a requirement to develop a specific microchip. They bring to their individual areas of design a perspective on such things as producibility, reliability, functionality, power consumption, operating speed, and cost efficiency. On the other side are the purchasers (users) of microchips, who are concerned with the whole chip—how it will fit into their systems and what portion of a given task the microchip will do. These are the people who are using microchips in producing medical equipment, computers, printers, cellular telephones, gas pumps, and so forth.

At Xilinx, a maker of microchips, the views of the designers and users are brought together so that the company makes a chip that users want. Peter Alfke, director of applications engineering, tells the designers what the users want and communicates to the users what Xilinx chips can do. This is not a simple task, as it requires good communication skills plus a solid technical background. Peter meets these requirements handily. He holds a master's degree in electrical engineering, has worked as a design engineer and design team manager for ten years, and has been in applications engineering for thirty years, either working alone or with up to one hundred people reporting to him.

Besides finding out what users want in new chips, Peter consults with users on any problems they are having using the company's existing microchips. His job is not a traditional engineering job, as he spends so much of his time writing and talking about his company's products and users. Nevertheless, without his engineering background, he would not be able to bring the different perspectives of designers and users together, and his company would not be making the chips Xilinx customers want.

Building Computers and Peripheral Devices

Computers are made of components typically manufactured and even partially assembled in a number of different locations before they are fully assembled. The same is true for peripheral equipment, such as printers and scanners. To a large degree, computer manufacturing has become truly global. In fact, a computer could be designed in one country, manufactured in another, and assembled in a third.

When a computer is manufactured, the components are assembled. Often this work is tedious, requiring both good eyesight and coordination, as many of the parts are very small. Although computer hardware assembly workers generally need only a high school diploma, they may need more specialized training than those who work in other manufacturing industries as this precision work can be extremely sophisticated and complex. For some assembly positions, certification in a technology or even an associate's degree in electronics or a related field may be required. A skilled assembler may put together an entire subassembly, or even an entire product, especially when products are made in relatively small numbers. Other, less-skilled assemblers often work on a production line, attaching one or a few parts and continually repeating the same operation. With increased automation, many assemblers—along with other production workers, including inspectors, testers, sorters, samplers, and weighers—are now doing more inspection work to determine whether the machines are operating as designed.

Earnings are generally high in production jobs in the manufacture of computer hardware. The average for all production workers is about $650 per week. Unfortunately, the demand for workers is expected to decline fairly significantly even though the world market for computers is relatively strong. The increased automation of assembly jobs, a rise in imports, productivity increases, and the moving offshore of much manufacturing are the main reasons for this expected decline in employment.

Selling Computers in Retail Stores

According to the Computer Industry Almanac, 27 percent of the PCs in use in the world are in the United States even though this country has only 4.6 percent of the world's population. While growth is expected to slow, the demand remains high for new computers offering the latest technology and fantastic new applications, from viewing movies to listening to music. Furthermore, people are no longer satisfied just having a PC; they want laptops and the ever-smaller computers coming on the market. In many homes, every family member has a computer.

The amazing growth in the number of PCs has resulted in an equally amazing growth in the number and type of stores selling

PCs. But this is not all these stores sell; they usually sell peripheral devices, from printers to mice. You will also find them selling an astounding number of accessories that help computers run smoothly, as well as supplies such as paper, CDs, disks, and printer cartridges. Many stores also rent, lease, and repair computers. Some offer training and consultations. Computer buffs can find a variety of jobs in computer stores and superstores, office supply stores, discount and warehouse stores, and mail-order and catalog firms. The opportunities for employment are good in this area, as there are more than forty thousand stores selling computers. In fact, you can even sell computers from kiosks in shopping malls.

While you won't need to have a degree in computer science to be a salesperson in one of these stores, you will definitely need to be knowledgeable about all of the computers in the store. And you will need to know how to talk to customers about what they need and find computers that will meet those needs. You should also be able to give demonstrations of the computer's capabilities. Once a sale is completed, you may need to arrange for delivery and installation of the computer and sometimes for the training of users. Part of your sales work is likely to include operating cash registers, accepting payment, preparing invoices, arranging financing, taking special orders, and stocking and arranging displays.

Because of high turnover in sales positions, it is not difficult for a skilled salesperson who is knowledgeable about computers and peripherals to get a job selling computers. Compensation varies with the store. You may receive an hourly wage, a commission, or some combination of the two.

Owning and Operating a Computer Store

There are now many ways to buy a computer, computer accessories, and peripheral devices. You can go online, go to a superstore selling all kinds of electronic gear, or visit a smaller local store. Some individuals like to buy a computer all packed up and ready in a box. Others prefer to have computers configured to their personal specifications. Most retail stores sell by the box.

Those who want a computer made to order typically go online or to smaller stores offering this service.

In the early 1980s, Alfonso Li went to a computer show and saw a booth that was labeled "franchising." Shortly thereafter, he was the owner of a MicroAge computer store. After some initial training, he opened his store and worked in both sales and repair with only two employees to help him. His business expanded into a larger store with twenty-five employees. This business took a lot of his time—it was decidedly not a nine-to-five job.

Every day on the job, Alfonso had to spend time learning more about computers. He read, went to seminars and schools, and talked to manufacturers. Technology was advancing so rapidly that Alfonso felt that everything would be changed if he took a six-month vacation and then returned to the computer business.

Alfonso was able to respond well to the changes in the computer retail business because of his strong business background. Besides having an M.B.A., he also worked as a corporate controller for seven years. The focus of his store changed as computers became so much cheaper and computer users so much more knowledgeable. With profits disappearing from the sale of PCs, Alfonso shifted more into selling high-end computers. He also greatly expanded services to customers in setting up and getting their computers running, including programming.

His store sold software and peripherals also. Because he could not find good technicians, Alfonso set up a school for technicians at his store. Successful store owners cannot just be computer buffs; they also must have a solid understanding of business and be prepared to work long hours.

More Jobs Involving Hardware

As the number of computers increases along with the complexity of these machines, so does the demand for people who can install, maintain, and repair this equipment. While technical degrees are not required for this work, job-seeking individuals are finding it increasingly helpful to gain certification. Also, more and more computer users are finding it necessary to use help lines to correct problems with their computers. The jobs of technical support specialists, computer support specialists, and the technicians who keep computers operating are described in Chapter 4.

Employment Trends

The computer industry is maturing. While growth is no longer as dramatic and downturns do occur, this industry is still expanding, and many segments actually experience significant growth every year as new products come out. Where jobs for hardware professionals were once concentrated at mainframe manufacturers, they now are distributed among companies that make computers and computer components, with more employees found at component makers. Demand should remain high for professionals in networking and communications fields as technology is changing so rapidly in these areas. And because products are becoming so complicated, an increased need exists for sales and marketing professionals and computer and technical support specialists with computer expertise.

For More Information

The rapid advances in computer technology are largely a result of the research, development, and design efforts of computer hardware engineers. For more information on careers, education, certification, publications, and conferences related to this engineering field, contact:

Institute of Electrical and Electronics Engineers (IEEE)
    Computer Society
1730 Massachusetts Avenue NW
Washington, DC 20036
www.computer.org

CHAPTER THREE

Software Careers

Once software is loaded into a computer's storage or memory, the computer can operate. It is software that brings hardware to life. Software guides shuttles into space and controls your microwave oven. Whether you use your computer to play video games, write a report, or create graphics, it is software that makes what you are doing possible. Software tells your computer what to do to perform these tasks. Software has had a profound effect on our lives in recent years. It is responsible for many of the recent gains in productivity. It has also changed how people throughout the world interact with each other by bringing us e-mail, instant messaging, and the Web.

Software can be divided into two major classes. Systems software runs the computer hardware and computer system. It includes operating systems, device drivers, programming tools, servers, windowing systems, servers, and more. Application software allows a user to accomplish one or more specific tasks. Typical applications include office suites, business software, educational software, databases, and computer games.

Working with Programs That Make Computers Run

Many individuals are involved in developing software and delivering it to retail stores, businesses, and other organizations. There are careers in software for engineers, programmers, salespeople, marketing experts, advertisers, teachers, trainers, technical writers, managers, and researchers, to name just a few areas. Customer service careers are described in Chapter 4.

Developing Software

The jobs of computer software engineers and programmers are often confused. It is the software engineer who creates the design of the software; the programmer creates the codes that make programs run. Software engineers apply the principles and techniques of computer science, engineering, and mathematical analysis to the creation of software. They can be involved in the design and development of either systems or application software. Computer systems software engineers coordinate the construction and maintenance of a company's computer systems and plan their future growth.

Software applications engineers analyze users' needs and design, construct, and maintain general computer applications software and specialized utility programs. While all software engineers need to have strong programming skills, they are more concerned with developing software than with actually writing code. Software engineers find jobs wherever there are computers, from start-up companies to established industry leaders.

Training

Most companies prefer hiring software engineers who have at least a bachelor's degree. Systems software engineers usually have degrees in computer science or computer information systems, while applications engineers have degrees in computer science or software engineering. Both engineers need to have a broad knowledge of as well as experience with computer systems.

It is easier to get an entry-level job by participating in internships and co-op programs while in college. Inexperienced college graduates may be hired by large computer and consulting firms that offer intensive, company-based training. In many firms, new employees have mentors helping them adjust to the demands of their jobs. Some firms hire individuals for systems engineering jobs who only have experience and professional certification. Because the software field changes constantly as new technology emerges, software engineers need to acquire new skills through continuing education and professional development seminars to keep up in this field.

Certification

Computer training programs leading to certification are offered by systems software vendors, including Microsoft, Novell, and Oracle. You don't even have to attend class to take the certification exam, nor do you need a college degree. There are study guides to help you prepare for exams. However, most experts think that certification alone is not enough for most software engineering jobs. Professional certification is offered to college graduates by the Institute of Electrical and Electronics Engineers (IEEE) Computer Society. To receive the certification, you need a bachelor's degree and relevant work experience and must pass an exam.

Skills

You definitely must have strong problem-solving and analytical skills if you want to be a software engineer. It is also necessary to be able to work closely and communicate effectively with team members, other staff, and the customers you meet. Because you must handle a number of tasks simultaneously, you must be able to multitask. And it's essential that you be able to concentrate and pay close attention to details.

Salaries

Computer systems software engineers earn about $74,000 per year, slightly more than applications engineers, who average about $4,000 less per year. The highest-paid systems engineers earn more than $80,000 working in scientific research and development services. The highest-paid applications engineers work with software publishers for $76,000 a year.

Computer Programming

Computers can do only what they have been told to do—which information to identify and access, how to process it, and what equipment to use. Programs vary widely depending upon the type of information to be accessed or generated. A program to update financial records is far different from one training a pilot in a flight simulator. Programmers write programs according to the specifications determined largely by computer software engineers and systems analysts. After the design process is completed, the programmer's job is to convert the design into a logical series of instructions that the computer can follow. The instructions are written in a conventional programming language depending on the purpose of the program. Many programmers use computer-assisted software engineering (CASE) tools to automate much of the coding process.

Besides writing programs, programmers also test the programs, debug the programs (correct errors), maintain and update the programs, and may even write the documentation (instructions on how to use a program or computer system effectively). On the job, programmers may work alone or be part of a group. They may be responsible for creating an entire program or just a segment of a program. It may take just a few minutes to write a program, or it may take years.

Computer programmers generally work in offices; however, more and more of them are now doing their work by telecommuting. While they are employed in every industry, most work in computer systems design and related services and in software publishing houses. No matter where they work, programmers spend long periods of time in front of computers.

Training

Professional programmers often have bachelor's or master's degrees in computer science. Increasingly, the associate's degree is becoming an alternative entry-level degree. Nevertheless, many excellent programmers have little or no formal instruction in programming. For example, many computer buffs regularly enjoy writing programs for their own computers. To gain professional expertise, they must learn how computer circuits are structured and should have a strong background in several programming languages. These languages have a fixed vocabulary and a set of rules that allow programmers to create instructions for a computer to follow. There are numerous programming languages, and no one language meets the needs of all programmers. Programmers generally know one or more of the following languages:

- Ada
- C++
- CASE (Computer-aided software engineering) tools
- COBOL (common business-oriented language)
- Delphi
- FORTRAN (formula translation)
- GUI (graphical user interface)
- HTML (hypertext markup language)
- Java
- .Net
- Pascal
- Perl
- PowerBuilder
- Prolog
- Verilog
- Visual Basic
- Visual C+++

Certification

While certification is not mandatory, it may give a job seeker a competitive advantage, since it is a way to demonstrate a level of competence. In addition to language-specific certificates that a programmer can obtain, product vendors or software firms also offer certification and may require programmers who work with their products to be certified. Voluntary certification is available through various other organizations, too.

Skills

Being a programmer requires an ability to pay extraordinary attention to detail. For example, just omitting a comma in an instruction can cause a system to fail. Programmers also must be able to think logically and concentrate on a task for long periods. In addition, they need to have stamina. Programmers may have to work long hours and go for days without much sleep when they are trying to meet deadlines.

Creativity is also an asset for programmers who must find unusual solutions to resolve difficult problems. And, of course, programmers must stay current on programming languages as well as the continual changes in technology.

Salaries

A large number of programmers are hired on a temporary or contract basis because companies often hire workers for a specific job and don't want to have to lay them off when it is completed. Such jobs can last from a week to longer than a year. The average earnings of all computer programmers is slightly more than $60,000 a year. The lowest 10 percent of programmers earn in the range of $35,000, while those in the highest 10 percent are able to garner close to $100,000 a year. A superstar programmer might earn as much as $150,000 a year.

Working as a Systems Programmer

Systems programmers write programs to maintain and control computer systems software, such as operating systems, networked systems, and database systems. They make changes in the sets of instructions that determine how the network, workstations, and central processing unit of the system handle the various jobs they have been given and how they communicate with peripheral equipment. Because of their knowledge of the entire computer system, they often help applications programmers determine the source of problems that may occur in their programs.

Job Requirements. Systems programmers need an extensive knowledge of operating systems. This includes being able to configure an operating system to work with different types of hardware. They also need the skills to adapt the operating system to best meet the needs of a particular organization. In addition, systems programmers must be able to work with database systems.

Career Path. Most systems programmers begin as junior or trainee programmers and receive considerable direction from project managers or team leaders. They typically advance to programmers, who receive less supervision, and then to senior systems programmers, who work independently. They can advance to project leader in charge of a team of programmers and to manager of operating systems with the responsibility for directing all activities of the department. The number of levels on the career path of a systems programmer depends on the size of the organization. Systems programmers do have a variety of career choices. Some elect to go into management, some choose to remain in programming, and others may move into systems analysis.

Working as an Applications Programmer

Applications programmers write programs that tell computers how to perform specific tasks, from billing customers to tracking inventory within an organization. They may also revise existing packaged software or customize generic applications called middleware. Applications programmers turn design specifications into computer code, which means putting the steps necessary to execute a program in a programmable language. The hot languages are currently .Net languages, such as APL, C#, and VB.Net. Applications programmers also debug and test programs and may write documentation. All of their work is user oriented rather than system oriented, like the work of systems programmers. They write programs that can be used on computers, from PCs to mainframes, and they work in a variety of places. They may be creating software at Microsoft, Netscape, grocery chains, banks, universities, research centers, or NASA; or they may be working by themselves at a mountaintop retreat. Wherever they are, applications programmers frequently work to create a product as part of a team of sales and marketing, documentation, training, and quality-control professionals. They often work in tense, pressure-packed situations trying to meet deadlines to finish a program on time.

Formerly, applications programmers developed systems from the designs of systems analysts. Now they work more closely with the users of their programs and often take over the design function as well. Thus, they may more appropriately be called programmer/analysts or software engineers.

Job Requirements. Programmers specializing in scientific or engineering applications need to have strong backgrounds in those subject areas. Programmers working for businesses may need courses in management information systems and business.

Career Path. Applications programmers work in two distinct areas: business applications and scientific or engineering applications. The career path in either area is similar to that of systems programmers. Applications programmers also begin as junior or trainee programmers, then they typically advance to programmer, senior programmer, project leader, and manager of applications programmers.

As for systems programmers, the number of intermediate steps in their career paths depends on the size of the organization for which they work. Applications programmers may change career direction and become systems programmers or systems analysts. Because applications programming is often the first job for those who are interested in information systems, many applications programmers ultimately take managerial positions.

Developing the Programs You Use—a Programmer's Story

When Fred Parsons sits down at a computer to program, he sees himself as an artist with the monitor his canvas and the keyboard his brush. Fred's first job as a programmer was at Timeworks, which produced education and productivity software. The company was one of the top one hundred producers of software in the United States at that time and had won awards for several programs.

As an undergraduate, Fred took only one computer course, a course in FORTRAN, and really enjoyed the programming part of the course. After graduating from college, he did not become a programmer but was a high school teacher for four years. The increasing number of layoffs occurring in teaching at the time convinced Fred to go back to college and work for a master's degree in computer science.

Halfway through the degree program, Fred started looking for work and found a job as a programmer/analyst at Timeworks. His first job was to write demos of programs that the company was selling so customers could see the actual screens from these programs in smaller software stores. It was a compiled BASIC (beginner's all-purpose symbolic instruction code) program. Fred was pleased with this assignment. The project manager would tell Fred what he would like to see and whether the job was going according to specifications. He also helped Fred with programming problems.

Career Path. With his next assignment, Fred began to climb the programmer career ladder. He was the only programmer on a team that included a writer, a packager, and people from marketing and advertising. All worked together under the direction of a project manager to produce a database program. The company told Fred what type of program he was to create and left some elements to his discretion. He had learned about databases in his graduate school courses in computer science but had to teach himself the programming language he used to create the database program. Logic and discipline from his undergraduate programming course and five or six graduate-level programming courses helped make this endeavor easier. Fred's experience clearly shows how helpful computer science courses can be to programmers in their work.

On the database project, Fred worked on the coding part alone and even did some of the design work. Coding involves writing down every single instruction the computer is to perform in a given computer language. For example, if a computer were to ask a question, it might take from one to one thousand instructions to make it ask the question in a user-friendly fashion. In coding, you write down certain key words or variables and mathematical equations; then a compiler turns your language into actual instructions for the computer in a language the computer can understand.

Once Fred's company saw that he could come up with ideas (programmers must be creative) and specifications, he advanced to the position of project manager and reported to the director of research and development. At one time, he was supervising four projects at once. Fortunately, the deadlines for the programs were staggered.

Changing Jobs. After several years, Timeworks went bankrupt, and Fred lost his job. This is a common occurrence in the computer industry, which computer buffs must face. After a short stint as a consultant, Fred elected to go to work at Comdisco, a technology services company that handled the design, acquisition, management, and protection of corporations' entire technology infrastructures. There, he worked on an asset management and procurement program for PCs that was so sophisticated it required a team of seven programmers. One advantage of this job was that Fred's hours were shorter, since he was working at a larger company that was not as dependent on the programmers to get the software out. Nevertheless, he was always working under a deadline—a situation that future programmers must anticipate.

Once again, Fred found himself working for a company that went into bankruptcy. As Comdisco employed fewer and fewer people, he even worked in human relations for a while before the company was bought by a German firm. This gave him an opportunity to travel to Germany and Vienna to train other programmers in the work Comdisco did. Subsequently, the German company split up the assets of Comdisco, and Fred went to work for a company called T-Systems, where he is today. Now his programming work involves updating and customizing an asset management database program. He is also in charge of the company's computer servers.

The Future. Fred says that programming is habit-forming—you get hooked on it—so he likes the idea of continuing to program. He also likes the idea of being in management, as he is more able to express his opinions as well as work with others. In any case, Fred says he never gets bored working in programming as the possibilities are endless, and there is always new technology to learn. For example, he learned the high-level language C++ when he first started at Comdisco by simply buying a book and going on from there. Fred strongly believes that there will always be a need for programmers, but he warns that industry downturns and company failures may require downsized programmers to seek new jobs.

Changing a Career Path

As a child, Adam Albert would sit and watch his dad upgrade computers. Then in high school, he took a keyboarding class and also played around with programming in Basic. These experiences helped him decide that a career involving computers was the right choice for him. At Purdue University, he majored in computer engineering, which was slanted toward the hardware side of computing but included some software classes so he felt that he could write code. Because he was part of the cooperative education program, he spent one and one-half years of his time at college working at Intel on a microprocessor. This work experience with hardware convinced him that this was not the career route he wished to follow. During his last year of college, he took some extra software classes and then attended a job fair, where he found his first job as a programmer.

Adam began his career at a start-up, where he wrote code for the company's product—a box that a computer plugged in to. It was used to transmit wireless messages between the computer and a server. For example, an ATM could be set up temporarily in a field so that fair customers could withdraw money. Unfortunately, this company folded, as did the next company, a consulting firm where Adam did a lot of Web page development using Visual Basic and Delphi programming languages.

Because the computer industry had fallen into tough times, he used a search firm to find his next job at a medical device company. His job there was to write code using C++ to make sure that IV pumps delivered medicine at the right rate. Lots of checks and balances had to be built into these programs. This was a large company, and Adam soon found that he had to sit around a lot while decisions were being made.

His current job is with a small health care firm that is a clearinghouse for insurance claims. Adam truly enjoys this job as it lets him be more than a programmer. He is now trying to create programs that automate claims submissions.

In the future, Adam sees himself remaining in active programming work rather than project management as he enjoys coding. He even taught himself C# to use in making his home-built jukebox work. Adam's career exemplifies the many opportunities computer buffs have to find the perfect jobs.

Debugging Programs to Make Them Work

Being a computer buff may run in some families. Rob Needham's father and grandfather worked with computers most of their lives, and he seems to be following in their footsteps. While Rob was attending college and working as a volunteer at a supplemental food program, a secretary asked him to look at a computer program that was giving her trouble. He looked at the program, saw where it failed, and contacted the program's developer at a local firm. After many conversations with the owner of the small company, CK Computer Consultants, Rob was offered a part-time job doing data-entry work. This led to a position as a quality-control specialist. The company specialized in software applications in the medical field and had just four employees.

Rob's basic job was to make the company's programs bulletproof. Any time a modification was made in one of the firm's programs, he had to check that program in a variety of ways to make sure that it still worked properly and didn't fail. When a new program was developed, he tried to "destroy" it (make it fail), and many times he succeeded. For example, in one program, patients were identified by their Social Security numbers or machine-generated numbers. Rob discovered that the same number could be given to more than one patient, which would have quickly corrupted the data. After he found this flaw, he described how he caused it and offered a solution. The owner, who designed all the programs, corrected the flaw, and Rob then retested the solution in several other ways. He also tried to re-create errors by taking a different approach. The process continued until Rob could no longer find any errors. In an eight-hour day, his error sheet might list as many as fifty or sixty errors to be corrected. Rob discovered far more errors in new programs than in existing programs that were being modified for new customers.

Because the company was small, Rob also did general office work and data-entry work for the company or the purchasers of the company's programs. When he worked outside the office doing data-entry work, he introduced the workplace staff to his company's program. At the same time, he also might find errors in the program. Rob says that he could test a program seven ways only to discover that the customers were using it in an eighth way.

For example, he discovered that some people have a habit of resting their hands on the space bar, which can generate errors. The company's program had to be corrected so that more than three hits of the space bar would not be acknowledged.

Rob is largely a self-taught computer buff, although he has taken courses in writing programs in FORTRAN and Visual Basic. He is fascinated by computers and would like to continue debugging programs, as well as get into programming directly.

Software Products Management

Companies that make computers also make or.buy systems software. Mike Tognoli is one of Hewlett-Packard's many product managers. Once he is assigned a new software product, a team is put together and a business plan is developed. His team negotiates with a number of different groups in Hewlett-Packard. For example, Mike must make sure that the new software is compatible with the systems on which it is designed to run. He also works with the group signing contracts with customers. The product must be marketed, which includes pricing and packaging. And, of course, it must be shipped to customers. In addition, Mike is concerned about service and maintenance of the product. This area is rather like a new-car warranty, as the company guarantees to fix problems with the software. Mike also spends time updating customers about the product.

Positions as product managers are usually held by individuals who have some business background. Mike says that managers tend to have or are working toward their M.B.A. degrees. In addition to an M.B.A., Mike has work experience as a financial analyst, a marketing manager, and an integrated-circuit buyer. The next step up the career ladder for product managers is to fully manage a larger group, rather than individual products.

Training People to Use Software Programs

When Ellen Leeb went to work at a new computer company, she was not a computer buff but a college graduate with a journalism major looking for a job. She took a job as a receptionist, promising herself to stay at that position only for a year as she looked for other job possibilities in the company. By networking with employees, she discovered an opening for a publications assistant in the software department and was hired for this position, proving that taking an entry-level job can lead to future job opportunities.

As a publications assistant, Ellen oversaw the production of three user manuals and eight technical documentation books. Her job was to coordinate the work of technical writers and graphic artists in producing the books. She also worked on having the books localized, which means translating them into different languages in such a way that they fit appropriately into the culture and business strategies of other countries. After a publication's firm acquired the company's training department, Ellen became involved with the production of training manuals as well as all the arrangements for training sessions for users and outside developers. Then she was promoted to a position in training where, in addition to overseeing the production of training manuals, she also managed groups of trainers.

In creating and producing software as well as hardware, many people are needed to handle administrative tasks. Ellen truly enjoyed being involved in the training of users and developers and appreciated the special atmosphere of the computer corporation, which respected everyone's individual work ethic. The company had no set hours and operated on a just-get-the-job-done philosophy, which made for a very dedicated, hard-working staff.

Selling Software

Just a few years ago, software was largely sold to consumers in retail stores, which included small stores and chain stores devoted to software as well as bookstores and computer stores. It was also possible to order software by mail. Today, most software is purchased at computer superstores, huge office supply stores, mail-order companies, and online. Each of these venues has a need for knowledgeable salespeople who can assist customers in the selection of the appropriate software to meet their needs. Computer buffs who are software gurus can get sales jobs without a college degree. In fact, it is even possible to work in sales part-time while you are still in school.

Software sales jobs certainly aren't limited to retail stores. Both small and large software companies must have salespeople. At the business level, this typically means selling a system that involves both hardware and software. While companies often train their salespeople, they also expect to hire people with considerable computer expertise and prefer employees who have degrees in computer science.

Technical Writers in the Computer Industry

When you want to know how to compute averages on your software spreadsheet program, you can easily find the answer by consulting your user manual. Programmers at end-user organizations use technical manuals when they are customizing programs to interface with their systems. Installers use manuals when they are implementing a system. These manuals are written by skilled technical writers who have a solid knowledge of computers and how they work. They also have the ability to talk with technical specialists about a product and then translate this information into language that nonspecialists can easily understand.

Education

Most technical writers have a college degree. Often, employers want them to have a degree in communications, journalism, or English. While a knowledge of computers is desirable, people with good writing skills can often pick up the specialized knowledge they need on the job, especially if they are computer buffs.

Salaries

Experience is very important in determining the amount of money that technical writers earn; so is location. The highest salaries are commanded in northern California and Massachusetts, with the average in these states exceeding $70,000 a year. The average salary for technical writers throughout the United States is more than $50,000 a year. Entry-level writers begin at slightly more than $40,000 a year. Independent contractors average more than $60,000 a year, but they have to pay for health insurance and benefits out of their wages.

Working as a Technical Writer

Although Betsy Morris graduated from college with a major in psychology, she has spent most of her career writing about how to use computers and training others to use them. In her first job with a start-up electronics company, she worked in production control buying parts and making sure they would arrive when needed. She then moved to a much larger company, where she continued to work in production control. That company brought in a new software system to organize production, and Betsy turned into a computer buff. She became quite expert at using the mainframe production software and soon was putting together computer manuals and holding training classes. This led to a full-time job as an engineering support specialist, which also entailed preparing materials for computer courses and writing a newsletter on the implementation of the new computer software.

After moving to a new town, Betsy answered a newspaper ad seeking someone to do technical writing and user support and was immediately hired for this position at a heavy-construction company. The company employed several programmers who developed software geared to the needs of the engineers and office staff in the firm. Betsy wrote manuals for the users and trained them to use the applications. She was also involved in selecting software and computers.

After a move across the country, Betsy made a decision to concentrate on technical writing in her next job. Although she liked to do support work, she felt it was difficult to be good in both areas as there were so many new technological developments to learn. Once more she found a job through a newspaper ad, this time as a technical writer for a software house producing very complex programs in the financial area. The programs were sold to large institutions such as banks and insurance companies. The learning curve was very steep at this job because Betsy had to learn not only about how each new program worked but also about the companies for whom she wrote the manuals.

On the Job. As a technical writer, Betsy usually works on manuals for two or more software programs at one time. The point at which she gets involved with a project depends on the project manager and her other commitments. If she is rushing to meet a deadline or has two or three manuals going at once, she cannot get involved in anything new until her schedule clears. Ideally she is brought in during the design phase and asked for input, but she often joins a project when this phase is completed. Because documentation has to be delivered a few days after the new software program, Betsy is busy writing the manual while the programmers are creating the program. She has to work closely with the programmers to get the information she needs for the manuals.

Demand for good technical writers is increasing. Today, there are more than the typical user, technical, and installation manuals to write. Technical writers produce security manuals, training manuals, and whatever the needs of the client and the complexity of the program dictate.

On one project, Betsy wrote all nine manuals. On other projects, she has shared the writing task with other writers. Also, the job of technical writer now extends to writing for and putting material on the Web. In Betsy's case, this even includes doing the graphics. Plus, in her job she often writes proposals and marketing materials.

Betsy wants to remain a technical writer because she truly enjoys the challenge of this work. She describes a good technical writer as an individual who is an excellent writer first and who also understands what he or she is writing about. Betsy sees no lessening in the demand for technical writers, but she does see a tendency in many firms to use contract writers when they need them rather than employing a large staff of in-house writers.

Employment Trends

Becoming a software engineer offers a very rosy future, as it is one of the fastest-growing occupations. While today's growth is not as rapid as in the previous decade, it is still very impressive as businesses and other organizations adopt and integrate new technologies and seek to maximize the efficiency of their computer systems. Plus, new growth areas will continue to arise from increasing use of the Internet and mobile technology, creating a demand for a wide variety of new products. Demand for software engineers may be somewhat tempered by an increase in contracting out software development abroad.

While demand for programmers will grow about as fast as the average for all other occupations, it is expected to grow much more slowly than that for other computer specialists. Jobs will be most plentiful at data processing service firms, software houses, and computer consulting businesses. Programmers are likely to face increasing competition from overseas, to which much routine work can be contracted out at a lower cost.

Demand for technical writers is increasing because of the rapid growth and change in the computer industry. There is a greater need for people to write users' guides, instruction manuals, and training materials.

For More Information

To learn more about what career in software is right for you, contact:

Association for Computing Machinery (ACM)
1515 Broadway
New York, NY 10036
www.acm.org

Institute of Electronics and Electrical Engineers (IEEE)
   Computer Society
1730 Massachusetts Avenue NW
Washington, DC 20036
www.computer.org

National Workforce Center for Emerging Technologies
Bellevue Community College
3000 Landerholm Circle SE, N258
Bellevue, WA 98007
www.nwcet.org

Society for Technical Communication
901 North Stuart Street, Suite 904
Arlington, VA 22203
www.stc.org

CHAPTER FOUR

Computer Services Careers

Every year, the number of computers in the United States grows. And every year, the complexity of computers increases. Keeping all these computers running, setting them up in homes and businesses, getting the right hardware and software installed, and using them to handle all kinds of data for businesses has created an enormous number of jobs. Few individuals or companies can now use their computers without some outside help from computer professionals. There are jobs for programmers, systems analysts, systems integrators, database experts, information systems managers, word processors, data-entry clerks, project managers, repairers, and customer support specialists. Providing computer services is projected to be among the fastest-growing occupations in the United States through the year 2012.

Professional Services

Large organizations have information systems departments that oversee the operation of their computer systems. Nevertheless, most organizations probably use outside professional services at times. They may need help in areas such as selecting new equipment, upgrading equipment, networking existing equipment, setting up a disaster recovery program, building firewalls, tutoring on-site, repairing equipment, or creating a new program. Organizations with a small staff of computer professionals use outside professional services for designing and implementing systems, customizing software, training staff, and repairing and maintaining equipment. In addition, individuals need outside help in setting up their computers. There is also a trend at present for organizations, large and small, to hire service companies to handle all or a great part of their information systems work. This is called *outsourcing*.

Integrating Systems

Service companies vary in the number of services they offer. The most important service today is systems integration. People who perform systems integration are called systems integrators. What they do is put together software and hardware components to meet a company's or an individual's needs. They may also run an entire computer system for clients. This is a big and growing business. Industry giants like IBM are offering systems integration services as well as many smaller companies and individuals working on a full- or part-time basis.

Jim Horio works part-time as a systems integrator at TJ and K Incorporated, the company he founded with Carl Lindke, who has now retired. When the two established the company, Jim knew a lot about accounting, and Carl was an expert programmer who had work experience as a systems engineer with IBM. Jim swiftly learned how to program with help from Carl by working on the S/32 computer in his apartment. Many of their company's first clients came from referrals by people they knew who worked at CPA firms. Their clients (small to midsize companies) were looking for new computer systems or to upgrade their current systems. Jim and Carl would analyze a client's needs, determine the hardware and software needed, and put the system together so it worked. They also wrote software programs, if needed.

Jim and Carl are telecommunications specialists, a skill that is in high demand today. Much of their early work involved installing telephone switches. They provided custom programming services to integrate telephone technology into computer applications programming. The two wrote programs that allowed telephones to talk to computers.

When they first started their firm, both Jim and Carl worked full-time at it. Then the emergence of the PC changed the nature of their work, and both took other jobs and did TJ and K work in the evenings and on weekends. After Carl retired, Jim continued to work and handled all of the company's business. Because he is a confirmed computer buff willing to spend much of his free time doing systems integration work, the company continues to be successful. One of Jim's major clients is a start-up, Cell Bio Sciences. Not only did he put together this company's computer system, he is also running the entire information technology department.

Career Advice. Jim advises individuals seeking to establish companies like his to get field experience in Windows server and PC set-up, installation, and configuration. He also believes it is helpful to be Microsoft certified.

Processing Services

Today's organizations have to process vast numbers of transactions and considerable data. They must handle payrolls, insurance claims, inventories, and numerous tax forms as well as perform many record-keeping functions. Some of these chores are routine, while others are large-volume, one-time projects. Even companies with large information systems departments are now having much of their large-volume transaction and data work done by processing services. Typically these services use their own hardware and software.

Processing services offer computer buffs such jobs as programmers, project managers, systems analysts, computer operators, database administrators, and data-entry clerks. They also employ numerous managers and salespeople.

A large data processing and accounting services firm provides a variety of services, while a smaller company might handle only one type of service. By looking at some of the services that a large firm offers, you can get a better idea of exactly what processing services these companies offer as well as the types of positions available for computer buffs.

- **Database Design and Management.** Staff members consult with clients regarding their needs and design databases that contain critical information used in conducting analytical reports and supporting marketing campaigns.
- **Tax Reporting.** The federal government requires companies issuing more than 50 1099s or 250 W-2s to report them on magnetic tape. This involves putting tax information on magnetic tape and providing firms with a duplicate tape as well as a printout of the contents.
- **Inventory.** The staff does customized inventory processing using custom programming to give retailers the output they need.
- **Data Entry.** On-site programmers customize each data-entry project. Then data-entry personnel quickly and accurately key it in for a quick turnaround.
- **Processing Services.** Some of the many services offered include transactional batch processing for large banks; large-volume, one-time projects; surveys; payment processing; and product registration.
- **Order Processing and Fulfillment.** Employees process the mail and telephone order business of various firms. Every order from arrival through delivery is tracked by computer.
- **Direct Marketing Support Services.** Staffers support customers' direct-marketing programs through data entry of customer names, response documents, orders, and registration forms; label production; list compilation and maintenance; order processing; direct-mail letters; and fulfillment services.

Information Services

Information services collect related information about a topic, organize it in a useful manner, store it in large databases, and provide online or off-line access to the information. This information usually can be accessed by computer twenty-four hours a day from wherever you are. The almost unquenchable thirst of businesses as well as individuals for information ensures the continued growth of this sector of computer services.

Information services may provide information on hundreds of topics or just a specialized topic. You can access information on such common topics as:

- business news and corporate profiles
- current news stories
- encyclopedia articles
- health
- market trends
- movie reviews
- sports updates
- stock quotations
- travel services
- weather

In addition there are databases with information designed for specific professions. Doctors now find out about new drugs and treatments by accessing medical databases. And lawyers are more likely to research case law through a legal database service than traditional law books.

Information Services Companies

Quite often when people think of information services, they think of industry giants such as LexisNexis, Dialog, and Dow Jones. These services store billions of records. However, there are many other large databases being operated by government entities, associations, businesses, and colleges. For example, the state of Indiana has the Learn More Resource Center that gives Hoosiers the necessary information and support to pursue and complete college. There are also small information services providing information for a particular customer niche.

Information Services Jobs

Computer buffs can find jobs in many areas in information services. There is a need for those interested in software and hardware to improve the technology in creating and distributing information. In addition, there are many jobs for customer service representatives and researchers. Individuals with database management skills especially are needed as the demand for information continues to increase.

Database Administrators. These administrators work with database management software and determine ways to organize and store data. They identify the requirements of the people using the database, set up databases, and test and coordinate modifications to the database. More and more, they are now planning and coordinating security measures to keep databases secure.

For this job, many companies look for individuals with a bachelor's degree in computer science, information science, or management information systems, and some want job candidates to have a master's degree in business administration with a concentration in information systems. As technology becomes more sophisticated, a higher level of skill and expertise is being demanded of job seekers.

Many database administrators find jobs with Internet service providers; Web search portals; and data processing, hosting, and related services firms. Others find jobs with the government, manufacturers of computer and electronic products, insurance companies, financial institutions, and universities. The average income of database administrators working for companies is about

$60,000. Those employed in computer system design and related services earn more than $66,000 a year.

Providing Technical Help and Support to Computer Users

Almost every computer user has encountered a problem occasionally, whether it is the disaster of a crashing hard drive or the annoyance of forgetting a password. The explosion of computer use has created a high demand for specialists to provide advice to users and customers when things go wrong as well as to install and repair both hardware and software. These support specialists may work either within a company that uses computer systems or directly for a computer hardware or software vendor. More and more of these specialists, however, are increasingly working for help-desk or support-services firms. Some have even established their own companies and work independently. Computer support specialists at hardware and software companies often enjoy great upward mobility; advancement sometimes comes within months of initial employment.

While there is no universally accepted way to prepare for a career as a support specialist, many employers prefer to hire individuals with some formal college education. For some jobs, a bachelor's degree in computer science or information systems is a requirement. For others, an associate's degree in a computer-related field is needed. Relevant experience, however, may substitute for formal education. In any case, the employer provides on-the-job training about users' problems and how to work them through these problems. Plus, continuing education is essential to keep abreast of all the changes in the computer field.

Help-Desk Technicians

When computer users run into problems that they cannot solve on their own or have a question that cannot be answered by reading a product's instruction manual, they typically call a help-desk technician. These support specialists field phone calls and e-mail messages from customers. In handling a request, technicians have to listen carefully to the customer, ask questions to diagnose the nature of the problem, and then patiently walk the customer through the problem-solving steps. For computer buffs who are intrigued by the challenge of analyzing and solving users' problems, jobs as help-desk technicians can be quite satisfying. You usually need to have a strong background in computer science coupled with an ability to devise creative solutions to diverse problems in order to handle these jobs. And, of course, you must be able to communicate effectively on the phone or by e-mail.

Job Outlook. The need for help-desk technicians is increasing faster than the average for all occupations as technology becomes ever more sophisticated and newer technologies emerge. Nevertheless, growth is this area is tempered somewhat as firms increasingly cut costs by shifting more routine work abroad to countries where workers are highly skilled but labor costs are lower. Physical location is not so important, as assistance can be provided remotely around the clock from anywhere.

Earnings. The average annual earnings of computer support specialists are approximately $40,000 per year. However, the lowest 10 percent of this group earns less than $25,000; the highest 10 percent earns close to $70,000.

Computer Support Services Firms

From large companies offering service across the nation on free phone lines to individuals moonlighting as consultants, companies have emerged to cover all the computer needs of users. Many companies only offer a single service, while others offer a wide range of the services, such as the following:

repairs	upgrades
installation	virus protection
disaster recovery	emergency data recovery
on-screen support	help lines
maintenance packages	tutoring
custom-built software	custom-built computers
firewall configuration	information system management

An Independent Tech Consultant

Believe it or not, Octavio Zuniga has been working in the computer industry since he was only fifteen years old. Because of his early enthusiasm for computers, he had acquired sufficient skills to work on the help desk at Earthlink in technological support answering callers' questions. One year later, at sixteen, he took a teaching position in a public school instructing gifted fourth and fifth graders after school on how to optimize their use of computers. Until he went to college, Octavio had never had any formal computer instruction. In college, he took computer information systems courses, and he also took courses at the companies where he worked.

Today, Octavio juggles work between his own company and his job as the only computer technician at a video and graphics firm. There, he does all kinds of work, from fixing printers and mice to working on customer files so they can go to print or film. In evenings and on weekends, he provides individuals and small companies with a wide range of services. Some of his recent jobs have involved helping an information technology (IT) department with networking, building a computer for an architect, helping people transition from old to new computers, repairing virus damage, and teaching the basics to first-time computer users. Overall, Octavio provides most of the services described in the previous section. In the future, he hopes to go out on his own and devote all of his time to his business.

Employment Trends

Opportunities are excellent for those who are interested in computer services careers as this is one area of the computer industry that is expanding rapidly. This is true even though some services such as help lines and the processing of large amounts of data are increasingly being handled offshore. While the number of jobs associated with computers grows steadily each year, the location of jobs tends to change rapidly. For example, many jobs are now found with outsourcing service companies instead of in company or government computer facilities.

For More Information

As the number of computers grows, so do the services that computer users want. For more information on careers providing these services, contact:

Association of Computer Support Specialists
333 Mamaroneck Avenue, #129
White Plains, NY 10605
www.acss.org

Association of Support Professionals
122 Barnard Avenue
Watertown, MA 02472
www.asponline.com

CHAPTER FIVE

Systems Analyst Careers

S ystems analysts have been defined as the designers and managers of the development of business applications. At times, they are called business analysts. No matter what name is used, these analysts are the key people who coordinate the computer systems of banks, insurance companies, consulting firms, financial services, manufacturers, government agencies, computer firms, and most large companies. Most systems analysts work with specific types of systems—business, accounting, or financial systems or scientific and engineering systems.

Three Functions of Systems Analysts

Systems analysts help computers do the work they are supposed to do at businesses and other organizations. They perform three different functions in their jobs. First of all, systems analysts work with users to find out what information the users expect the computer to generate. Systems analysts are also investigators who gather facts about existing systems and then analyze them to determine the effectiveness of current processing methods and procedures. This phase may also include preparing a cost-benefit analysis of the current system. Finally, they are architects who plan and design new systems, recommend changes to existing systems, and participate in implementing these changes. Being able to handle the three distinctly different roles of a systems analyst requires certain characteristics. If becoming a systems analyst interests you, take this quiz to see if you have most of the requisite traits.

- Are you self-motivated and creative?
- Can you work equally well with technical personnel and those with little or no computer background?
- Are you tenacious—able to stick with a problem until it is solved?
- Can you handle a number of tasks simultaneously?
- Do you have the ability to concentrate and pay close attention to detail?
- Are you able to think logically?
- Can you deal effectively with difficult people?
- Are you a team player?
- Are you a good listener?
- Are you interested in a wide range of subjects?
- Can you communicate effectively both orally and in writing?
- Do you possess the ability to coordinate activities among many levels in an organization?
- Do you have good organization skills?
- Do you have a broad knowledge of computer systems?
- Are you familiar with programming languages?
- Are you a college graduate?
- Do you have an analytical mind?
- Are you self-disciplined and self-directed?
- Are you able to work for long periods even if there are few tangible results?
- Do you enjoy attending meetings?
- Are you willing to write numerous reports—even when there has been little accomplishment?
- Can you manage time and resources effectively?

If you answered yes to most of these questions, you probably possess the personal qualities and skills to become a successful systems analyst. Your work will be with computer systems, which are made up of people, machines, programs, and procedures all organized to accomplish certain tasks. Organizations have systems because a system is an orderly way to get things done. For example, colleges have systems to register students in the classes they want. These systems have such components as registration forms filled in by the students, lists of available classes, registration personnel, and computer programs.

How Systems Analysts Work

Whether your task as a systems analyst is to create a brand-new registration procedure for a college or to improve the system for regulating the air temperature inside the space shuttle, your project will usually have six phases. How many systems analysts will be involved in developing and implementing a new system and what their individual roles will be naturally depend on the complexity of the system as well as the analysts' expertise.

The preliminary investigation is simply a brief study of the problem to determine whether it warrants further investigation. The systems analyst handles this phase primarily through personal interviews with end users who have knowledge of the problem as well as the system being studied. This phase is usually quite brief. At its conclusion, systems analysts usually give management a report of just a few pages telling what they found and giving their recommendations.

The systems analysis phase involves gathering and analyzing data from interviews, written documents, questionnaires, and personal observations. This phase takes a lot of legwork and time and can be quite expensive. Once all the data have been gathered, it is time to analyze them using such tools as organization charts, data-flow diagrams, grid charts, data dictionaries, and decision logic tables. The final step is to make a report to management that details what problems were found, gives possible solutions, and recommends what the next step should be.

The systems design phase involves the planning and development of the system's operations. Systems analysts begin this phase by finding out exactly what information must be produced by the system (output). Once they know what the desired output is, they have to determine what is required to produce it (input), how the data will be stored, and how the system will operate to produce the desired information. An important part of this phase is to develop system controls to ensure the data are input, processed, and output correctly. This phase concludes with a detailed presentation of the system to management and users and, perhaps, with approval to begin developing the system.

The systems development phase begins with the scheduling of all the activities that have to be performed. Then design specifications have to be prepared for all the programming that will be done, including the selection of the programming language. After the programs have been written, the next step involves testing to see if all the programs work together satisfactorily. Finally, documentation is required to describe the programs for operations personnel and users of the system.

The systems implementation and evaluation phase indicates that the system is ready to operate. Systems analysts must evaluate whether everything is working as planned. The reliability of the system must be tested and necessary modifications made. In addition, the changeover from the old system to the new involves training personnel.

The systems maintenance phase begins when the development process is concluded. Changes have to be made to correct errors, give the system additional capability, or react to new needs of the users.

Working as a Systems Analyst

It helps to have a little bit of Sherlock Holmes in you in order to be a successful systems analyst. You must investigate until you find out exactly what an end user really needs and wants. This often takes some time as many end users are not able to express precisely their computer needs. You also must be a teacher willing to help reluctant users learn to feel comfortable with computers and computer technology. Furthermore, you must realize that you are changing a familiar system and may find that some end users are reluctant to embrace or even antagonistic about these changes. Tact is absolutely essential in working with these people.

Computer analysts must wear many hats as they work on devising new systems or modifying older ones. At times, they need to be salespeople in order to sell new technology. Besides interacting with people, they must be skilled professionals who can choose the correct hardware and software and design systems that meet the needs of an organization and its end users.

A Systems Analyst at a Small Insurance Firm

Ann Steefer has always been interested in computers. When she was a little girl, her parents put basic spelling games and word games on their old Apple computer. While she enjoyed playing the games, she was continually thinking of ways to improve the screen graphics, layout, and performance of the game. When it came time for college, Ann went to Purdue University, where she obtained a B.S. degree in computer science.

Today, Ann is a systems analyst for small systems at the insurance firm where she started as a basic programmer and later became a programmer/computer analyst before advancing to her current position. She oversees the development and support of a PC application that is used for placing orders over the entire nation. There are three programmers on her team.

In her job, Ann has continuous contact with the people in her firm who use the application in order to know what their needs are and how their needs are changing. Biannual meetings help her determine what changes and improvements need to be implemented in the system. Ann prioritizes this work and delegates it to her team members. Depending on the complexity of a change, Ann may develop program architecture to assist the programmer or work on the code herself. Ann has always enjoyed working with the development of applications and does not want to let her technical skills go unused.

In this continuously changing field, Ann finds it difficult to keep abreast of all the newest technology. She takes classes offered through her company and local computer vendors on new applications and future products to keep her skills current. Ann also reads computer magazines.

A Systems Analyst at an Army Finance Center

David Charles is a true computer buff. "The computer has great appeal to me," he says. "It enhances me." His interest in computers grew as he saw computers becoming so popular in the workplace and in homes. David truly enjoys spending his leisure time at home on the computer. He handles most of his correspondence using word processing and graphics packages on his PC. And the bleak winter months find him playing educational games on his computer.

David climbed the career ladder to his present position as a project manager for small systems though a series of jobs. He started as a basic programmer and subsequently became a programmer/ analyst, a section leader, and a department leader. His current job consists primarily of managing a tax-input system (PC-based, from external offices to a central-site mainframe computer). He writes procedures for system users, analyzes problems, and advises personnel at troubled sites. David also is a team chief responsible for nine systems analysts working in many subject areas within the military pay system.

David believes that as a systems analyst you are more marketable if you have management experience, which also can help you, in some instances, to negotiate a better salary. He likes the opportunities that are open for him in the future, which include either continuing to work for the government or moving to a large corporation. His advice for future systems analysts is to get a sound educational background and be careful not to become overspecialized in one area because the technology is continuously evolving.

A Systems Analyst at a Major Manufacturer

In high school, Denise Jatho not only expressed interest in the computer field to her counselor, business teacher, and math teacher, she also read books on computers and the computer field. Her math teacher, who served as a mentor, worked with the local college to enroll her in a computer course. After taking the college course, Denise decided to attend the university to get a bachelor's degree in computer science. Since the computer industry is always in flux, she takes an average of two weeks of training every year through the company where she works.

Today, Denise works as a team leader in the commercial systems and services department of corporate information services for a manufacturer of heavy equipment. Because the user base for the software Denise develops is distributed worldwide, her workday usually begins by answering any e-mail or telephone messages from company people in different time zones, from as far away as Switzerland and Singapore. Next, she checks her organizer for meetings throughout the day. Denise usually averages one meeting each day with users, her team, or special committees. Skills for interacting with people are essential to success in her position. It is as important for her to have a team that works and bonds well together as it is to have a good relationship with her manager.

Denise's primary job is to develop and support PC software for business-unit users in her company. Throughout the day she assigns tasks to members of her team. She also assists them with problems they have encountered or provides any training required to complete an assigned task. She may also work on the development of new software and enhancements or changes to software. During the day, Denise receives approximately ten calls from users and other software developers in her company to discuss software support issues. As a team leader, she also has the responsibility of making sure her manager is up-to-date with what Denise's team is doing and any problems that have come up.

One of the main reasons Denise enjoys her job is because it is challenging. She has to be both creative and logical in her thinking. She finds it's like working with one big puzzle that is always changing; once she has successfully completed one piece of the puzzle, the next one is waiting. Because the field is in a constant state of change, there is always something new to learn, so she is never bored. Denise also gets the chance to teach and coach other people and see them progress and grow, which is extremely rewarding to her.

Career Advice. Denise advises future systems analysts to research this career through reading and talking to people in the computer field. She also suggests going to technical fairs, if possible. In addition, Denise believes it is important to find a mentor— someone you respect who can help you learn and grow.

Education Requirement for Systems Analysts

At present there is no course of study that will completely prepare an individual to become a systems analyst because employers have such different requirements. Not only are they seeking college graduates with degrees in some aspect of computer science, they also want their successful job candidates to have course work related either to business or to the area in which they will be working. For example, graduates who have an education background in physical sciences, applied mathematics, or engineering are preferred for work in scientifically oriented organizations. Furthermore, many systems analysts have M.B.A. degrees, which give them the additional expertise in business required for many analyst positions.

If you plan to enter this field, you need to realize that continuous study will be required as technology is advancing so rapidly.

This can be accomplished through in-house training, vendor courses, college classes, and seminars. It can also be important for you to obtain certification. You can find out more about certification by contacting:

Institute for the Certification of Computer Professionals
  (ICCP)
2350 East Devon Avenue, Suite 115
Des Plaines, IL 60018
www.iccp.org

Climbing the Career Ladder

Almost all systems analysts begin their careers as programmers. After approximately two years, they may advance to positions as programmer/computer analysts or senior programmers. This is where they gain customer-interaction and management skills before being promoted to a systems analyst position. At this point, they may decide their next step up the career ladder is to senior systems analyst, where they have more managerial responsibilities, or to technical support analyst, which involves more programming. The career route of many analysts leads to positions in information systems management or senior management. Some experienced analysts may start their own computer consulting firms.

Employment Trends and Salaries

Systems analysts have favorable job prospects as this is one of the fastest-growing occupations and one that is not easily outsourced overseas. Close to half a million people work as systems analysts, and this number should grow steadily. The average salary of systems analysts is more than $60,000 a year. The lowest 10 percent earn less than $40,000, while the highest 10 percent earn more than $90,000.

CHAPTER SIX

Computer Operations Careers

The job world of computer operators is changing rapidly from what it was in the heyday of mainframes that filled rooms as large as basketball courts. It was not too long ago that large staffs were required to operate the mainframe computers that many companies were using. They had to input the information through punched cards, mount and remove magnetic tapes, and handle the printed output from the computers. At that time, computer engineers sent by the manufacturers performed preventive maintenance almost daily. As computers have become more powerful and sophisticated, entering and storing data are much easier tasks. In fact, it has become so easy to input data that end users are handling most of this work themselves rather than data-entry personnel.

While computer operations staffs are now smaller at most facilities, workers are still needed to keep computer systems running. Their jobs, however, have changed greatly. Sophisticated software, coupled with robotics, enables a computer to perform many routine tasks formerly done by computer operators. Scheduling, loading and downloading programs, mounting tapes, rerouting messages, and running periodic reports can be done without the intervention of an operator. As technology continues to advance, the responsibilities of many computer operators are shifting to areas such as network operations, user support, and database maintenance. Operators are definitely not the only people involved in the operation of computer facilities, however. There are also careers for those involved in setting up computer software and hardware environments that allow the systems to run smoothly, especially in the area of networking.

One interesting aspect about operations is the possibility of working in shifts or on weekends or even part-time. Since computers at many organizations run twenty-four hours a day, seven days a week, there can be a need for the operations staff to work around the clock. However, shift work is becoming increasingly unnecessary as automated operations let the computer itself take over operations during less-desirable working hours. In addition, advances in telecommuting let some operators monitor the operations for the next shift from off site.

As organizations have come to rely more and more on the information generated by their computers, the importance of the smooth and reliable operation of computer systems has increased. It is easy to understand why the Internal Revenue Service, nuclear power plants, transportation systems, airline reservations systems, and many other organizations need solid performance from their operations staffs.

Working as a Computer Operator

Who are the computer operators? They are the individuals responsible for the operation of computer systems. Computer operators work directly with computers. Their duties vary with the size of the installation, the type of equipment used, and the policies of the employer. Generally, operators control the console of either a mainframe digital computer or a group of minicomputers. They work from operating instructions prepared by program users or operations managers. Operators typically have the following duties:

- set controls on the computer and on peripheral devices required to run a particular job
- make sure the equipment is in running order

- load equipment with tapes, disks, and paper as needed
- monitor the computer console
- execute procedures at the right time
- respond to operating messages
- locate and solve problems or terminate a program
- retrieve, separate, sort, and distribute program output
- assist end users with routine operational problems such as not being able to sign on
- document key activities and unusual events during a shift
- help systems analysts and programmers test and debug new programs

As the trend toward networking accelerates, more operators are working with local-area networks (LANs) and/or wide-area networks (WANs), which serve multiple servers (computers that manage network resources) and personal computers. Operators also work with servers that provide many client computers with access to files, printers, and application programs as shared resources to a computer network. Think of the networks as data pathways by which PCs communicate with servers.

Advancement

In the past, computer operators frequently got their training on the job. Today, more employers are looking for operators who have had formal training from vocational and technical schools, community colleges, the armed forces, or computer manufacturers. Constant learning to keep up with advancements in technology through reading and specialized courses is essential.

Only a few computer operators can expect to advance to supervisory jobs. Opportunities are best for those with formal education, such as bachelor's or master's degrees. Through on-the-job experience and additional formal education, some computer operators may advance to jobs in network operations or support. By gaining experience in programming, there is also the possibility of finding positions as programmers or analysts.

Salaries

The average earnings of computer operators are around $30,000 a year. The lowest 10 percent of operators average less than $19,000, while the highest 10 percent earn more than $46,000. Operator salaries are generally higher in large corporations than in small ones. For example, the average earnings of those employed by the federal government exceed $41,000 a year.

A Computer Operator at a Government Facility

At a large government facility, large mainframe systems have been slowly replaced with servers. Servers are much more powerful and take up very little space. Customers from all over the country, and even the world, access the data stored on the server twenty–four–seven. The server, a Hewlett-Packard 6400 computer, is located at a server farm in a different state. This server farm has machines from a variety of vendors. A server can be partitioned into areas for development, testing, and production. The computer operator has been replaced by the database administrator (DBA). The DBA is very versatile. He has worked on the design of the server so the purchase of the complete system maximizes the efficiency and scalability required by the usage. Once the system is installed, he monitors all aspects of the system to keep the operation running smoothly. For example, he looks at how much of the central processing unit is being used. If there are too many users on the machine, he tweaks the server so it runs at maximum efficiency.

Frequently, users write queries (requests) for certain information. Some may write very inefficient queries, which can cause a drain on the system. One user requested twenty million records to generate a report on his PC. When the DBA saw what was happening, he cancelled the query. The information about the user and some suggestions on how to best develop the query are passed to the Operations Team. The Operations Team contacted the user and helped the user modify the query so that it would give the desired information and would not make the database inaccessible to other users.

Computer Operators at a Large Investment Bank

Accurate record keeping and quick transaction processing are absolutely necessary at an investment bank. For example, traders must be able to access at once how many shares of a particular stock are owned by the bank. Also, they must be able to quickly process trades done for customers. To handle the several hundred thousand transactions that are done every day, this bank has floors devoted entirely to networked computer servers. In each area, operators (called technicians) monitor what is going on. Should a particular computer experience a physical malfunction, they either remove and repair it or remove it and install a new one. These operators have limited responsibilities because the computers are so sophisticated. For example, some computers monitor whether the other computers are operating as they should. If not, the monitoring computer may be able to correct the problem. Also, when problems come up on some of the computers, the computers are actually able to send out messages to the technical staff responsible for their operation.

While this investment bank still has a number of mainframe computers employing operators, most computing is done either by servers or by desktop workstations. All of these machines are connected to the network throughout the firm, which lets them communicate and share information.

Supporting Computer Operations

The PCs, printers, telecommunications devices, and other computer equipment found in organizations have to be serviced and maintained. Some organizations have this work done by outside service organizations. However, many organizations have technical support specialists on their staffs to keep their computer systems up and running smoothly. These technicians install, modify, and repair computer hardware and software. They also work on monitors, keyboards, printers, and mice. Some may write training manuals and train computer users how to properly use new computer hardware and software.

Beginning technicians usually have some training in electronics or electrical engineering. They typically get their training from vocational and technical schools, junior colleges, the armed forces, or on-the-job experience. And as technicians climb their career ladders to more supervisory positions, they usually take specialized courses.

Job opportunities are increasing faster than for most occupations as more sophisticated help is needed to keep computers operating around the clock. The average annual salary for technical support specialists is close to $40,000.

Technicians working with hardware need to have good manual dexterity and patience as well as the ability to communicate with computer users. Take the following quiz to see if you possess the skills needed to be a technician:

- Do you like to fix and install things?
- Are you a good listener?
- Can you ask questions to obtain information from others?
- Do you enjoy figuring out why something is not working?
- Do you have good powers of observation?
- Are you able to work under pressure?
- Do you enjoy working with tools?
- Can you handle working with people who are irate?
- Do you have an interest in computers?
- Are you willing to keep up-to-date on different systems?
- Are you physically strong enough to lift heavy equipment?
- Do you enjoy reading?

Having a career as a technician is definitely a hands-on job. You need to enjoy tinkering with equipment and have the persistence to locate and solve users' system problems. You also will constantly be required to read manuals to update your knowledge.

Supporting the operation of computers also involves individuals who do the paperwork involved in purchasing, repairing, and maintaining computer systems. In addition, many technicians find themselves doing far more than maintaining and servicing computer equipment, as you will see in the following interviews.

Working as a Technical Analyst

Michael Holtz worked as a technical analyst at the Toledo Hospital. Michael felt good about his job because he was able to save the hospital money. He knew that they were getting his services cheaper than if they were to hire someone outside the hospital to repair computer equipment, as he did far more than computer repair work.

Michael took the first step on his computer career path in 1983 when he applied for a scholarship to the Ohio Council of Private Colleges and Schools. He wanted to enter the computer hardware technology field. Michael received the scholarship and was granted full tuition in the ten-month program.

After graduation, Michael began working at Abacus II, a retail store that not only sold computers but provided technical support to customers. As a bench technician he had the responsibility of taking in CPUs (central processing units) and repairing them. After a year and a half in this slot, he went to a branch store, where he was the only person providing the needed support for customers who purchased equipment from this store. He held this position for a year and then was promoted to head technician at the corporate store, where he supervised three technicians. Michael left this position to do on-site computer repair for large corporations that the company serviced. He stayed at this job until he began working at the Toledo Hospital.

Michael was the only technical analyst at the hospital. His duties included keeping the hardware running, repairing computers, keeping track of repair costs, purchasing necessary parts, doing paperwork for repairs and purchases, and providing assistance on the operating systems and the software programs. He assisted four systems analysts, which included giving them his recommendations on new systems they selected to purchase.

On the job, Michael was usually involved in a wide variety of activities. Here's what one day's accomplishments included:

- completed weekly time sheet that showed where he had spent his time in the hospital
- installed a new printer and moved equipment
- spent some time installing another hard drive in a system that needed more drive space
- spent two hours with the systems analysts who identified the users who would be adding or upgrading programs

After working for several years as a technical analyst, Michael became a network analyst and then a network server specialist at the hospital.

Working as a Network Administrator

As the role of computer operator changes due to new technology, the responsibilities of many operators have shifted to working with networks. Network administrators work with both the hardware and the software of computer systems to ensure they run properly and are compatible with other programs operating on the network. They may also work on designing new computing devices or computer-related equipment and software to make the end users' interaction with the input of data as error free as possible. Network administrators need to have many of the same personality traits and skills as computer operators, but they typically earn higher salaries.

A Network Administrator at a Major Manufacturer

Wade Bishop is a network administrator in the computer operation department of a major manufacturer. He is part of a seven-person team that services the network computer needs for more than twenty-five hundred users locally and eight hundred other users throughout the world. His background includes taking computer courses in high school, working in the U.S. Air Force with computers, and studying computer science in college. While in school, he concentrated on the networking aspect of computing. This involved learning how everything fits together, both with hardware and software. Through courses in PC architecture, PC LAN technology, and systems analysis and design, he gained many of the networking skills he uses today. Wade has found that strong analytical skills for problem resolution and good interpersonal and communication skills are also prerequisites for success in his job. According to Wade, you have to like to learn if you work in networking because today's solutions to problems will be obsolete in eighteen months.

Daily Schedule. Upon arriving at work at 6:00 A.M., Wade first checks all of his messages via e-mail, voice mail, and cell phone. Then it is time to start dealing with the problems reported by users to his area. Next, he checks back-up runs for completion and initiates any failed jobs after fixing all errors.

Every day, Wade and his project leader try to sit down to discuss all current problems, fixes to problems, or new and upcoming projects. The remainder of his day is spent working on projects and resolving problems for users as they arise. Since Wade interacts with more than twenty users each day, he doesn't spend much time at his desk, as he usually goes to the user's desk to look at the problem.

Working in Data Entry

Data-entry workers are the people who input data into computer systems or complete forms that appear on a computer screen. They also may manipulate existing data, edit current information, or proofread new database entries for accuracy. They often work with medical and insurance records and membership lists. The basic criteria for obtaining a data-entry position are speed and accuracy on the keyboard. Clerical skills such as answering the phone, typing, and filing also may be essential. You can prepare for this position by taking high school or vocational school courses. Use the following quiz to determine whether you have the necessary traits to be a successful data-entry worker.

- Can you easily follow directions?
- Do you mind sitting for an eight-hour day?
- Are you able to concentrate in a room with other workers?
- Are you able to work with little supervision?
- Do you like idea of inputting information into a terminal?
- Do you have good keyboarding skills?
- Are you able to cope with the pressure of deadlines?
- Can you handle working in front of a computer screen all day?

Yes answers to most of the questions indicate that you could probably handle data-entry work. Often, this is a person's first job after graduating from high school. It also can be a stepping-stone to higher-paying jobs with increased responsibility. It is very common for data-entry workers to be promoted to supervisory jobs assigning work to other data-entry workers and making sure the data-entry department is running smoothly. The average annual income in this field is more than $22,000 a year. Data-entry workers employed by the federal government and large organizations can average as much as $25,000 a year.

From the following interview, you will learn more about the tasks of data-entry workers and discover what additional responsibilities they may be assuming in this job.

Data-Entry Clerk at a Small Business

Kim Reed took only one computer class in high school, a basic programming course; however, her jobs have involved working exclusively on the computer. On her first computer job with the public defender's office, she spent five hours of her eight-hour day typing legal documents and correspondence. Her on-the-job training was in using a word processing program. After two and one-half years in the public defender's office, Kim went to work as a data-entry clerk for a window and door company. The company has five outlet stores selling quality windows and doors and a main office where she works as the company's sole data-entry operator. Kim spends her day working on two different systems: the company system and the factory system.

Kim's workday begins when she receives a printout of all the files that she entered the day before on the factory system. She checks to make sure that the files have come back from the factory the way that she entered them. Kim then goes through all the orders that have been faxed in overnight and makes decisions about any changes that have occurred. At this point, Kim opens the sales journal in the company file and logs in all jobs, construction types, sales representatives, and amounts of money.

The next step in Kim's job is to pull up customer files, make any necessary changes in individual files, and to create customer files for new jobs. The next file that Kim works on is order maintenance, where she enters order headers and creates documents from the orders listing all products that have been purchased by the customers. After printing everything she has entered in the computer, she staples each printout to the order and gives it to the individual who will prepare the orders for the factory system. Kim's work for the morning is now completed.

After lunch, Kim spends the next few hours on the computer working on the factory system. She returns to the order maintenance file, creates order headers, and types in information for the orders needed from the factory. Before Kim leaves the factory system, she prints out all the order data that she has entered and sends the orders to the factory. The final hour in her workday is spent doing additional data-entry work, making phone calls, answering questions, and printing copies of contracts. You can see that Kim's job description as a data-entry clerk involves considerable decision making and is not just inputting data.

Kim says that her job has taught her about the importance of the computer to the operation of her company. She enjoys typing and having the same daily routine. Kim says she is good at what she does because she does it every day. Over the years, she has gained speed and accuracy because she knows not only the codes but also the system. Kim accepted a new job with the company in the order department because she wanted the additional mental stimulus of a more demanding job. Once again, the job of data-entry clerk was a stepping-stone to career advancement.

Employment Trends

Overall employment of those who truly have hands-on jobs with computers is declining. The expanding use of software that automates so many jobs that computer operators once did has sharply reduced the need for operators. Opportunities in this area are best for those who have formal computer-related education, are familiar with a variety of operating systems, and keep up-to-date with the latest technology. The employment picture is the same for data-entry workers. Their numbers will decline as various data-capturing technologies are used to input information into computers. Also, as telecommunications technology improves, more and more data will be transmitted electronically and entered automatically into computers. In addition, data-entry work can be done in other countries by workers who are paid lower wages.

CHAPTER SEVEN

Information Systems Careers

I t's absolutely essential for organizations from colleges to banks to manufacturers to use the latest computer technology in order to remain competitive. The responsibility for handling this task falls on the information systems or technology departments of these organizations. The history of information systems is a brief one, going back to the days when systems and procedures departments set up courses of action for the efficient use of paperwork and employees.

Today's information systems departments revolve around using the computer to develop and provide information to the staffs of organizations from the federal government to your local fast-food restaurant. They are frequently referred to as information technology departments. When organizations first started using computers, they were usually placed in data processing departments and used to handle bookkeeping and inventory functions. These departments were typically run by data processing managers, who were considered technical experts by the senior managers, who really did not know much about computers or computer applications. At the same time, data processing managers were often inept in communicating to management the more sophisticated ways computers could be used in their organizations. The job of data processing manager was considered to be a dead-end job, not an avenue for advancement to the top management of an organization.

As computers became cheaper and more powerful and as a wide variety of software packages became available, companies started using computers for more than just mundane tasks. Computers were elevated to the realm of running the business of the organizations, and managers used them to order shipments, purchase inventory, and make decisions. The position of information systems manager evolved to coordinate the needs of management for computer information with the rapidly expanding capabilities of computers. And the term *information processing* came to be used for *data processing* in many organizations.

Information Systems Manager

The manager of information systems has the responsibility of efficiently and effectively directing the operation of the computer systems on which an organization depends, plus providing the employees with the information services they need. Information systems managers typically have the following job responsibilities:

- keeping abreast of trends and advancements in hardware and software technology
- evaluating new technology for possible use in the organization
- analyzing the present and future computer and information needs of the organization in consultation with senior management
- developing a plan to meet the organization's information needs
- planning and coordinating such activities as the installation and upgrading of hardware and software, programming and systems design, development of computer networks, and implementation of Internet and intranet sites
- directing the work of systems analysts, computer programmers, support specialists, and other computer-related workers

- implementing appropriate back-up and security measures
- creating a budget for the operation of the systems information department
- training personnel in the information systems department
- assigning and reviewing the work of department employees
- reporting on the status of all information systems operations to senior management
- staying in touch with the activities of the organization
- serving as a buffer between personnel in the information systems department and those outside the department

Where Information Systems Managers Report

Since most organizations introduced computers in the accounting area, it was quite common for managers of information systems to report to the controller or vice president of finance. In many businesses this is still true today. However, as the importance of information systems to organizations grew, the title of chief information officer (CIO) was created, and information systems managers became part of senior management, reporting to the executive vice president, president, or chief executive officer.

When you think of the important role the information systems department plays in the success of such organizations as airlines, banks, insurance companies, and credit card companies, it is quite easy to understand why in many organizations the manager of this department is given senior management status in charge of the overall technological direction of the organization. At the same time, the information systems department in a small company may have only one employee.

The Career Path to the Top

As long as computers were primarily used to handle basic processing applications, the manager of the computer department tended to have a technical background. Today, individuals who are selected to head information systems departments may come from either a technical or a managerial background. In either case, managers of information systems departments must demonstrate communication skills that enable them to speak to users without overwhelming them with computerese. They also must have a thorough knowledge of the organization for which they work. Typically, information systems managers have several years of experience working for an organization before they are selected to head an information systems department. A possible path to the top, which includes both technical and managerial experience, is as follows:

- programmer
- systems analyst
- project manager
- first-line manager
- second-line manager
- chief information officer (CIO) or top manager

Leading the Information Systems Department of a Food Company

International Multifoods was a leading processor and distributor of food products to food service, industrial, agricultural, and retail customers in the United States, Canada, and Venezuela before it was acquired by the Nestlé Company. Paul Taylor was the organization's first vice president of information services. Paul was very familiar with International Multifoods operations, as he had been responsible for the performance of one of the company's major operating divisions involving ten plants, one thousand employees, and $300 million in annual sales.

Although Paul had impressive managerial experience, he had absolutely no technical computer background. He did know, however, what he wanted the corporate information services department to do for the division that he recently headed. Furthermore, his division had been the company's largest user of the corporate data center resources.

Top management selected Paul for the position of vice president of information services because the company needed someone to turn around the computer operations. The department had not been meeting users' needs. Thus, Paul became the company's first vice president of information services—a position that reported at first to the office of the chief executive and later to the chief financial officer. The corporate data processing department and all related operations were incorporated within the new information services department.

Paul's first task in his new position was to acquire the technical knowledge he needed, which he did by attending classes and seminars. During Paul's six and one-half years managing the information services department, he developed a coherent long-term strategy to ensure that the computer function of the department was meeting the needs of the users and that the corporation was making effective use of the available computer technology resources. Paul oversaw the building of a data center after recommending this major capital expenditure to the board of directors.

After the data center was built, a mainframe was installed. Later, the mainframe was shut down, and servers were installed in corporate headquarters. The tasks formerly done by the mainframe were given to an outside service bureau. In addition, Paul decentralized computer operations so that the department at corporate headquarters did not have direct responsibility for the operation and maintenance of the computers in remote operating divisions. These divisions just sent in month-end consolidated financial information. The payroll operation, however, became centralized and was handled by the outside service bureau. By the time Paul left this position to work as an executive with a custom-printing service bureau, he had met the challenge of his assignment by making the computer operations responsive to corporate needs.

Directing the Installation of a New Computer System at an Art Museum

When the Asian Art Museum of San Francisco with its fifteen-thousand-piece art collection moved from its location in Golden Gate Park to the former Main Library, a new data and telecommunications system needed to be installed. The individual chosen for the job as director of information technology was Jim Horio, an experienced programmer and systems integrator—careers described in earlier chapters. Jim also had gained experience as a program manager and was managing the information systems for a manufacturing firm that built high-tech pumps for instruments before taking the job at the museum. This was an extremely challenging job, as the museum wanted the computer system to handle inventory, accounting, membership, ticketing, gift shop transactions, and building maintenance. It also wanted to have multimedia kiosks scattered around the museum that visitors could use to learn more about the exhibits. Later on, these demands extended to the building of a website that would give site visitors an opportunity to look at items in the collection. What made this job even more challenging was that all these tasks had to be accomplished within a reasonable price tag, as the funding was a combination of public bonds and private donations.

Fortunately, Jim had the experience, contacts in the computer world, and ingenuity to meet these demands. To provide the computer power essential for all the applications the museum wanted, he had to adapt equipment from the old museum and design and purchase a largely new computer system. He chose the midrange servers produced by IBM. Then, to meet the challenge of creating a searchable online database of selected art museum pieces, he chose the Linux operating system. This was one area in which Jim did not have much prior experience, so he took a Linux class. It is important to remember that no matter what experience you have, you will constantly need to stay on top of new technology in order to handle almost any job in the computer world.

Although there were many last-minute snags, including a two-month delay in moving to the site and the arrival of the videos for the kiosks only two days before the opening of the museum, the computer system was up and operating on opening day. Jim's job as IT director is definitely less hectic now. However, he is constantly faced with new challenges, such as stopping school children from hacking into the system through the kiosks and developing an application so online visitors can check their art interests and then receive a mailing for upcoming events that will interest them. Plus, as IT director he is always tweaking the system so it will meet new applications demands.

The Job of Second-Line Managers

The information systems departments of many organizations have large staffs composed of project managers, programmers, systems analysts, network operators, computer operators, database analysts, maintenance workers, and many other employees. Second-line managers are usually in charge of a specific function of the information systems department and the staff supporting that function. They report to the chief information officer and may advance within a few years to this position. Although organizations vary greatly in their number of second-line managers and the functions that they handle, the following chart illustrates some of the positions commonly found at this level. Of course, job titles differ from organization to organization.

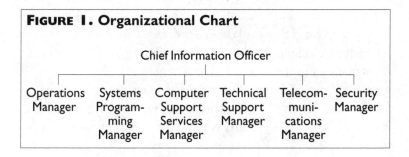

FIGURE 1. Organizational Chart

Chief Information Officer

| Operations Manager | Systems Programming Manager | Computer Support Services Manager | Technical Support Manager | Telecommunications Manager | Security Manager |

Education

While there is no universally accepted way to prepare for managerial positions, employers are increasingly preferring these individuals to have a bachelor's degree in computer science or engineering. For significant upward mobility, an M.B.A. or an M.S. in computer science is a definite asset.

Operations Manager at a Retail Chain

The job of operations manager is to direct and control the operation of all computer and peripheral equipment of an organization. The more essential the operation of computers is to the success of an organization, the more important the position of operations manager becomes. Just imagine the financial cost to an airline if the computers are down for more than a few minutes. Think of the dangerous situation that can occur if computers are not operating properly at nuclear power plants. Contemplate the confusion that occurs at banks, insurance companies, and brokerage houses when their computers are not working.

Bill Needham was the operations manager for the information systems department of an upscale retail chain with more than seventy outlets. One of the minimum requirements for being an operations manager is having a good knowledge of hardware, software, and operating systems. Bill amply met these requirements by having almost thirty years of work experience at IBM after graduating from college. His jobs at IBM ranged from education and marketing to systems engineering. While working as a systems engineer at IBM, Bill learned of the opening for an operations manager at the retail chain. He decided to take advantage of the early retirement program IBM was offering to become operations manager at the chain's headquarters.

In large organizations, operations managers may have many section managers and supervisors reporting to them. At the retail chain, Bill had four operators who were responsible for the operation of an iSeries computer. Throughout the day and evening, the point-of-sale equipment in the company's outlets sent records of all transactions to the iSeries, plus the time and attendance records of employees. The computer was also used to keep track of sales and inventory and to generate a variety of reports for management.

Bill reported to the vice president of information systems and had responsibilities similar to those of most operations managers. Because his department was small, and because of his personal interest in programming, he spent more hands-on time working on the operation of the computer system than do other managers. Nevertheless, looking at Bill's major responsibilities will give you a good idea of the type of work this position entails:

- reporting to management on the status of the system, including how close to capacity and speed it is operating
- ensuring adequate computing capacity is available to handle the work
- handling equipment breakdowns so downtime is minimized
- keeping up-to-date on new technologies and how they apply to the company's system
- installing new software to update the system
- putting new equipment in retail outlets, which involves selecting, evaluating, testing, packing, and sending equipment to the stores
- negotiating some contracts with outside vendors for maintenance, supplies, and other services, such as off-site microfiche storage
- staffing the operations department, which includes hiring, firing, and training operators
- checking operator logs to see if the operators are handling the problems of store personnel correctly
- working on disaster preparedness plans

Since the trend in many organizations is to decentralize computer operations and put personal computers on users' desks, the need for operations managers is not likely to increase significantly. Still, this position remains important in systems management because downtime can be disastrous for many organizations. Bill, whose interest in computers goes back to his childhood when his father worked for IBM, believes opportunity for advancement in this position lies in becoming vice president of information systems or moving to a company with a larger operations staff.

Programming Manager at a Cruise Line

You have just read about Jim Horio's job as director of information technology at an art museum. One of his jobs along the way to this top position was as the programming manager at a cruise line. Before this, he had worked in the information systems departments of corporations, while at night and on weekends he worked at home on projects for his own computer firm. You learned about Jim's company in Chapter 4.

While working as a contract programmer several years ago, Jim saw a newspaper ad for a senior programmer with a major cruise line. Lured by the possibility of taking reduced-price cruises, Jim applied for and obtained the job. As a senior programmer, he designed, modified, and wrote new applications programs and worked on user programs for accounting, reservations, and purchasing on two IBM midrange computers. Within one year Jim was asked to become the programming manager, a second-line management position that reported to the manager of information systems. Besides programming, Jim now had the additional responsibilities of assigning work to the company's six junior and senior programmers, prioritizing assignments, and seeing all the work was done on time—typical responsibilities for a programming manager. Jim's rapid ascent up the information systems career ladder continued as he became a manager of information systems reporting to the vice president of finance one year later.

When the cruise line moved its operations from California to Florida, Jim decided to leave the company. Nevertheless, he had fulfilled his original dream by taking cruises to Alaska, Japan, Europe, and the Caribbean, including a working vacation programming an IBM midrange computer aboard a ship.

Division Manager of Information Systems at a Very Large Corporation

Bill Fisher's father encouraged him to get a degree in business so he would have the skills needed for a successful career. This has proved to be solid advice, as Bill has used the skills he learned getting a B.S. in marketing and an M.B.A. along with technical training to swiftly climb the career ladder in information systems at a large Fortune 500 corporation. After a two-year stint in the U.S. Army, Bill became a trainee in information services at the company where he is now a division manager of information systems.

Career Path. Bill's technical training at the corporation began with an eight-week course that covered all the fundamentals of systems. His first assignment was on financial systems. After only four months, he was moved to another product area, where he supported and developed marketing-related systems for two years. His next move was to the information service training group, where he taught technical courses and helped the company with recruiting for five years. Then Bill was promoted to the position of senior analyst, becoming part of a team developing systems to manage high-rise warehouses.

After three years with the group, he became a project leader and one year later, a supervisor. As a supervisor, he left the technical area and returned to marketing, becoming responsible for a team that developed various marketing systems. His next step up the career ladder was a promotion to information services manager in Geneva, Switzerland, where he stayed for four years until returning to corporate headquarters and his present position.

On the Job. Bill has started a group that is responsible for all systems that support his company's ordering process. He finds that he spends the majority of his time in meetings. He meets with his staff members regarding projects and personnel issues; with end users concerning projects, visions, and changes; and with other personnel in information services about the information technology and product direction that should be pursued. A great deal of Bill's work revolves around the 110 people on his team who work in smaller teams to accomplish the tasks of his unit.

Career Advice. Bill believes that solid organizational skills are required to be a successful systems manager because so many demands are placed on your time. He also suggests developing your communication, technical, and decision-making skills.

More Second-Line Manager Positions
Here are several more jobs at the second-line management level:

- **Technical support managers** have the responsibility of finding new and better ways to use equipment and meet users' needs. In many organizations, the functions of this position are handled by the chief information systems officer or other second-line managers.
- **Telecommunications managers** are in charge of the efficient transmission of information for organizations that are geographically dispersed. They also are responsible for the installation and administration of local-area networks (LANs) and wide-area networks (WANs). These managers direct the networks and their related computing environment, including hardware, systems software, applications software, and all other computer-related configurations.
- **Security managers** are increasingly found in second-level management. Their primary responsibility is to protect information in the computer system so that unauthorized

persons cannot examine, copy, or alter it. They plan, coordinate, and implement an organization's information security. They may also educate users on computer security, install security software, monitor the network for security breaches, respond to cyber attacks, and, in some cases, gather data and evidence to be used in prosecuting cyber crime.

Employment Trends and Salaries

Organizations are increasingly placing a greater value on information and expanding their information services. Demand for computer and information systems managers is growing much faster than the average for all occupations. Because technology continues to boost the employment of computer-related workers, the demand for managers to direct these workers is also increasing. An interesting trend has developed recently in which companies have a job candidate work on a project or contract basis in order to evaluate his or her work before hiring the candidate on a full-time basis.

Demand is especially strong in two areas. Many organizations are actively looking for individuals who can keep a computer network running smoothly. And the emergence of cyber security as a key issue for so many organizations has greatly increased the demand for managers proficient in computer security issues. Opportunities for top management (CIO) positions are best for job candidates who have an M.B.A., with technology as a core component, or a management information systems (M.I.S.) degree, along with advanced technological knowledge and strong communication and administrative skills.

Salaries continue to increase for top-level managers of information systems. Those employed at organizations earning the highest revenues tend to have the highest salaries. Table 1 shows the current range of salaries for information systems managers.

TABLE 1. Information Systems Salaries for Management

TITLE	SALARY RANGE
Chief Information Officer	$114,000–$191,250
IS Manager	$80,250–$112,250
Manager, Applications Development	$75,750–$105,750
Manager, Technical Services	$59,000–$85,000
Manager, Telecommunications	$64,500–$84,500
Senior Manager, Operations	$61,000–$83,250
LAN/WAN Administrator	$47,000–$68,500

Source: Excerpted with permission from Robert Half Technology, 2884 Sand Hill Road, Menlo Park, CA 94025.

CHAPTER EIGHT

Computer Careers in Special Areas

T he lively commercials that you see every day on TV, fantastic animated films like *Shrek*, and almost all the special effects in movies are done by skilled artisans working on computers. Musicians are now creating, recording, and manipulating sound on the computer, too. And it is not just the entertainment world the computer has changed. Everything—from bridges to stadiums to overcoats—is being designed on the computer. In plants throughout the world, the computer is out on the floor helping in the manufacture of cars, tools, planes, and thousands of other items. Computers have absolutely revolutionized the way so much is done in the world.

Designing with Computers

The lower cost and increased power of computers plus the design of sophisticated software packages have led to the common use of computers by designers, whether they are architects, engineers, interior designers, or other design specialists. Today's homes, cars, planes, refrigerators, toasters, and furniture all are being designed on the computer. So are magazines, newspapers, corporate reports, brochures, and other publications. Computer-aided design (CAD) enables the design and technical drawing of projects on a computer. It involves the use of both software and special-purpose hardware. At first, the use of CAD was confined to large automobile and aerospace companies. You now find designers in small offices and homes creating designs on powerful PCs. CAD is swiftly replacing designers' drawing boards no matter what they are designing.

To use CAD, the designer can begin by scanning in an existing design, can use elements of designs provided in design programs, or can use the computer to create a design. Throughout the design process, the designer makes changes by using the command functions of the CAD program. For example, lines can be shortened, lengthened, curved, erased, moved, and so on, and sections of the design can be moved around. The design can even be viewed in 3-D, and a part can be rotated to produce multiple views of it. When the design is finished, it can be stored for reuse or future modification. The design also can be reproduced with a printer or a plotter that uses special pens to draw the design.

Training

As CAD is used in so many different careers, the training requirements vary. Many individuals are self-taught, while others have studied CAD at colleges and technical schools. On the job, most CAD users constantly update their skills by interacting with coworkers as well as learning new programs.

A Project Designer Using CAD

After working for two commercial interior design firms, Dawn Jones started her own company, DJ Design. Her offices are in her home, where she has two computers set up on AutoCAD and a plotter to plot drawings. She subcontracts other designers who do CAD work to help out with drafting and space planning.

The primary focus of Dawn's company is facility management. One of her clients is a major consumer electronics company, where she works with the real estate and facilities operations departments to coordinate requirements of growth with other departments and to look at the entire master planning for the campus of buildings. One of Dawn's primary tasks is to keep all the floor plans for these buildings up-to-date on CAD. Keeping track of approximately 650,000 square feet, just in Indianapolis alone, plus five plants in Juarez, Mexico, and El Paso, Texas, has proven to be more than a full-time job. So Dawn spends considerable time working on-site at the firm.

Dawn's company also does tenant space planning for developers of such facilities as medical offices, hospitals, and restaurants. Developers who lease space come to Dawn's firm requesting a space plan for tenants or prospective tenants. First Dawn meets with the tenant to ascertain the tenant's needs. Once she knows the tenant's space requirements, she does the actual design work on the computer. Her task is much simpler if the plan of the building is already on CAD. Then Dawn simply finds the plan and proceeds with her space design. If the building plan is not on the computer, she has to go out and measure the building, return to the office, and draw the shell on the computer before she begins her actual space plan. Her completed space plan is shown to the tenant. If the tenant likes her plan and the brokers and leasing agents come to an agreement, Dawn does the construction drawings. This involves such things as showing where walls, restrooms, and storage areas will go. She also does an electrical plan and a finish plan, which has details about wall coverings, carpets, and other finishing touches. All of her plans are done on the computer. After the design is approved by an architect and the necessary permits are obtained, Dawn supervises the construction.

Dawn gained her expertise in designing space while working for her degree in environmental design at Purdue University. Even though she had taught herself CAD in high school by doing the tutorial and reading the manual, she took three CAD courses in college. On the job, Dawn continues to learn more about CAD from her coworkers, who have different specialty areas in which they excel. Dawn would like to continue doing space design work. She sees an ongoing demand for individuals who can do this work, as so many developers want the plans for older buildings to be on CAD. Although the initial drawing of a building is not much faster with a CAD program than with pencil and drawing board, the CAD plan is more accurate and can be revised quickly.

A Civil Engineer Using CAD

Bob Stallard is an assistant project manager for Granite Construction Company. Although Bob primarily uses CAD for developing charts and graphs for presentations, the civil engineers who work for him use it for all their construction drawings of roads and bridges. Most of these engineers are self-taught because the CAD systems are so complicated. The engineers must do the tutorials and then learn all the options and possibilities by solving real problems.

Bob considers the computer a valuable aid that facilitates the production of drawings. It replaces the normal drafting tools, such as pencils and protractors. For example, to draw a circle, the engineer does not use a compass but instead keys in the radius and specific coordinates. By using the computer, the engineers in Bob's department are able to make precise—not just accurate—calculations and drawings. They also are more productive because drawings can be swiftly revised, a process that is both slow and expensive when done on the drawing board. Besides assisting engineers in their drawings, special CAD programs can be used to analyze their designs. CAD helps engineers answer questions: What is the maximum weight a bridge can hold? What is the most efficient design for a cloverleaf? And so forth.

Drafters Use CAD

Drafters are the people who prepare technical drawings and plans used by production and construction workers to build everything from manufactured products, such as toys, toasters, industrial machinery, and spacecraft, to structures, such as houses, office buildings, and oil and gas pipelines. They fill in the technical details, using drawings, rough sketches, specifications, codes, and calculations previously made by engineers, surveyors, architects, or scientists. Traditionally, drafters sat at drawing boards and used pencils, pens, compasses, protractors, triangles, and other drafting devices to prepare a drawing manually. Most drafters now use CAD or computer-aided design and drafting (CADD) systems to prepare their drawings. The drawings are stored electronically so they can easily be revised and duplicated.

Drafters still need the knowledge of traditional drafting even though they use computers. Most have completed training at technical and community colleges. After initial training, they take course work in a specialty such as aeronautics; architecture; civil, electrical, or mechanical engineering; or electronics.

Manufacturing with Computers

The age of computer-aided manufacturing (CAM) is here. And robots are no longer just starring in movies; they are out in the factory doing innumerable tasks, from working in hazardous situations to performing the same job over and over until they are reprogrammed.

The automation of factories continues to accelerate as does the demand for professionals who can design and implement these automated systems. Sophisticated CAD/CAM systems work together so that the design is developed on the computer and then sent to computer-aided manufacturing equipment.

An Engineer Working with CAD/CAM

Greg Lyon works at Aircom Metal Products, which manufactures products through sheet metal fabrication and plastic injection molding. Many of the parts produced by Aircom lend themselves to the use of CAD and CAM. Greg, who is an electrical engineer, spends considerable time designing parts using CAD. He learned how to use the company's system by reading manuals and observing an experienced CAD user.

Greg uses the customer's part drawings and specifications to develop a tool design and draw it on the computer. Then a CAM expert, who is also a machinist, determines what aspects of the drawing can be machined by computer-controlled equipment. Because there are many different types of computer-controlled machines hooked directly to the CAD/CAM system, the CAM expert must choose the appropriate piece of equipment. After a machine is chosen, the CAM expert uses the computer-aided machining software to generate the program code, which is sent to the machine via serial cable. After minimal setup, a machinist can begin to produce the tooling designed to make parts according to the consumer's specifications.

Not only does Aircom's CAD/CAM system save considerable time and money, it also has increased quality through increased accuracy. In the years prior to CAD/CAM, these same tool designs would have had to be hand drawn and machined using calculations performed by the machinist.

Today, with the computer's assistance, a piece can be drawn and machined accurately within four decimal places (.0001 inches), and the software is continually getting better. According to Greg, CAD/CAM is now the cornerstone of manufacturing, and companies must use it to be competitive.

Graphic Design with Computers

Computer have revolutionized the field of graphic design, enabling designers to work much faster and more efficiently than in the days of hot typesetting and cut-and-paste layout. The software programs for graphic design and page layout continue to evolve, bringing new tools and greater flexibility to the designer's desktop. As with CAD/CAM, the constant new developments require graphic artists to make continuing education a priority.

Learning to Be a Graphic Designer

Sarah Craven is a talented artist who always took art courses in high school and college. After college, she attended a postgraduate school to learn graphic design with the ultimate career goal of becoming the art director of an advertising agency. Sarah did not spend her time at school learning how to draw layouts by hand. Instead, she worked almost exclusively on the computer. In her classes, she learned how to use several graphics programs, all with different capabilities. Out of class, she worked on her own to master the programs. This involved working with a copywriter to create layouts and designs for print ads. Whatever she could visualize, she learned to do by manipulating images on her computer screen using a mouse or the keyboard. The only limitation she truly faced was having enough computer memory. Sarah has discovered that the more you know about computers, the more likely you are to be hired in today's job market. Since graduation, she has spent her days on the computer working as an art director on several national ad campaigns.

Computer Animation

Computers have changed the way animation is done. In fact, many current movies could not have been created without the techniques that have been developed in computer animation. Although some animators are self-taught, many receive computer training at art or design colleges or schools.

Before entering the job market, animators create portfolios that let prospective employers evaluate their work. Animators typically work for movie and television studios, advertising firms, and software companies.

A Computer Animator

Don Bajus is an animator who has made some imaginative commercials that you might have viewed on television. Today he has a new tool—his computer—to help him animate. Don can now animate in 3-D and light the characters and a scene as if they were real. The computer knows where the objects and the characters are as well as their dimensions and can compute where the highlights fall and where to cast the shadows. If a client wants a different camera angle, it is no longer a task requiring weeks of work. The animator can change the camera position, relocating it by moving the camera or altering the viewpoint. The lighting can also be changed in a similar way if needed.

Don can move characters in the computer using software that walks a character rather than drawing every movement as in traditional animation. The computer can make these changes easily compared to cel animation. In cel animation, every movement is a series of drawings made up of key position drawings and in-between drawings. It is the same process in computer animation, only the animator moves the character into key positions, such as in a walk sequence where the first key position could have the left leg on the ground and the right leg lifting. The next key position could have the right leg outstretched ready to come down, the left leg moved back, and the body leaning slightly forward. The animator creates all the key positions and then lets the computer do the in-between positions. This is not an easier task than cel animation because of the difficulty of the dimensional concept. However, having the computer insert the in-betweens can be time-saving if enough good key positions are used.

Now it is also very easy for 3-D computer animators to change colors as the characters are each a single element throughout the production. In cel animation, characters represent twelve to twenty-four separate drawings per second, and in the past these were finished on cels (sheets of celluloid film) with inked or copied lines and paint.

In the new computer paint software, colors are added through a paint program and can be adjusted quickly or changed completely, unlike traditional hand-painted cel animation. It's just a matter of touching the cursor to the paint palette to pick a new color, then moving the cursor to the area to be changed and pressing the cursor again, and every frame in that scene will have the new color in the chosen area. In cel animation, this kind of change could take weeks. By using the computer for 2-D cel painting, the benefits include the ability to add textures, have constant-density shadows, and create automatic drop shadows.

New 2-D software programs let Don either draw on paper and then scan the drawing into the computer or draw directly on the screen. From there he can paint the drawing. He can also swiftly move characters in or out of a scene or from the foreground to the background. The backgrounds, foregrounds, and characters are on separate levels, and each level can be moved independently in any direction. This allows for the multiplane effect, as with a zoom-in, where multiple levels of objects pick up speed as they move closer to the viewer—something very complicated in cel animation. The more sophisticated animated commercials seen today are most likely created by animators like Don using computers to produce them.

Computer animation technology is advancing so rapidly that programs are becoming more capable each year. Don believes the main advantage to using computer animation is the ultimate control it gives the animator over each and every item in the scenes. He sees very exciting days ahead for animators as the computer programs become more user friendly. In the future, he would like to produce his own animated short stories using the emerging technology.

Learning to use a computer for animation can be quite frustrating, according to Don. "At first, the computer won't do anything you want," he says. "But as you gain skill, it will do almost whatever you want." Don is glad that he was an animator before he started to use the computer because he can think beyond the obvious things the computer can do to assist him in his work. Although there are schools teaching computer animation, Don believes that you should become an animator first so you will truly understand what animation is and will realize that the computer is just a tool—an expensive, powerful, and sometimes obstinate "pencil."

Computer Musicians and Technicians

The computer has invaded the music world. It is being used in composing, recording, and manipulating music and sound. One person with a computer can produce the sound of a symphony orchestra or a rock band. Musical computer buffs often work in the entertainment arena creating music for movies, games, CD-ROMs, videos, and other multimedia products. Some compose music while others work on the technical side, mixing and editing the sounds. Computer musicians often work for production studios, record companies, and music publishers, but many freelance.

Training

Formal training is not a prerequisite for a career making music on the computer. Many have learned the technical aspects of computer music through on-the-job experience and are self-taught musicians. Nevertheless, as more jobs in music involve computer technology, those with formal technical training will have an advantage in the job market.

Creating Music on a Computer

If Johann Sebastian Bach were alive today, he would probably be composing on the computer. Just as Bach wrote music to order for patrons, Doug Benge, owner of Bengemark Music Works, is creating music for clients, usually advertisers.

The first step involves talking to the client to find out what the music is to accomplish—the desired mood or image. Then Doug uses a computer program as he composes a piece of music. The musical notation program transmits what he plays on a keyboard to notes that he can see on the computer screen. Then, without leaving his chair in front of the computer, Doug is able to assign his newly composed piece to different synthesizers using two software programs to compose the music in a rough form.

The client listens to the music, and any necessary changes are made before the final product is recorded. Just as Doug creates music on the computer, so do other musicians throughout the world.

The Marriage of Entertainment and Computers

Anyone who has seen movies recently is aware of the wide use of computer-generated special effects. In Hollywood, a great number of small firms are emerging to meet the demands of filmmakers who want to put the extra zing of special effects into their movies. Even the giant studios are setting up in-house departments to develop new film techniques. And these techniques can be used to save money.

For example, the computer can turn a herd of ten charging bulls into one hundred or, with just a little work from computer animators, can eliminate the need to send actors to exotic locales for filming. The public's demand for evermore exciting special effects in films will lead to an increasing number of jobs for imaginative computer visual effects and software creators.

Games are not just appealing to children; adults spend hours playing them on computers and entertainment systems. After all, these games are fun. You can enjoy the challenge of all types of games, from poker to sports to solving mysteries. Besides playing video and computer games, computer buffs can find jobs creating the software for games as well as the hardware to operate them.

A number of small companies are emerging to produce not only interactive entertainment but also educational materials. Jobs in interactive media are available for computer buffs who are graphic designers, software programmers, and hardware creators as well as those interested in sales, marketing, and management positions.

Employment Trends and Salaries

Computers are now an important tool in design, manufacturing, animation, music, and entertainment, and their importance will continue to grow. While the number of computer-related careers is expected to increase, employees in areas like manufacturing and graphics arts will find that job opportunities are closely tied to cyclical changes in the economy. As far as the arts go, this is one area in which computer buffs can combine their love of the computer with their special talents.

The salaries of drafters vary by specialty and level of responsibility. Most drafters earn an average salary of about $40,000 a year, with a few earning almost $70,000 a year. Illustrators earn average salaries of more than $35,000 a year. Motion picture and video animators have average earnings of close to $60,000 a year, while graphic artists average about $37,000 a year.

For More Information

Information on schools offering programs in drafting and related fields is available from:

Accrediting Commission of Career Schools and Colleges of
   Technology
2101 Wilson Boulevard, Suite 301
Arlington, VA 22201
www.accsct.org

Information about drafting career certification is available from:

American Design Drafting Association
105 East Main Street
Newbern, TN 38059
www.adda.org

For general information about art and design and a list of accredited college-level programs, contact:

National Association of Schools of Art and Design
11250 Roger Bacon Drive, Suite 21
Reston, VA 20190
http://nasad.arts-accredit.org

For information about graphic design careers, contact:

American Institute of Graphic Arts
164 Fifth Avenue
New York, NY 10010
www.aiga.org

CHAPTER NINE

Internet Careers

People are online at work, schools, and libraries. You see them online at coffeehouses and cybercafés. You find them walking around using BlackBerries to access the Net. Soon, they'll even be using their computers online in planes. It's no wonder that you see people online almost everywhere, as almost 70 percent of the people in the United States are Internet users. Even though the Internet is very young, it is now a career destination that is offering computer buffs a wide array of new jobs because of the myriad ways in which it is being used. While the number one use is e-mail, the Internet is also being used for its information resources, shopping, games, educational activities, and services ranging from checking a bank balance to planning a trip. All these uses translate into a great variety of job opportunities for computer buffs, whether they are interested in hardware, software, or operations jobs to those in marketing, accounting, or writing. As you read this chapter, learn more about Internet companies and employment opportunities by visiting the websites given in the text.

Providing Access to the Internet

Providing access to the Internet has resulted in an intense competition among access providers to sign up new customers. From technicians to software engineers, from service representatives to marketing professionals, there are jobs for skilled computer buffs at all of the companies providing access to the Internet.

Where the Jobs Are

Many different companies provide access to the Internet. There are jobs with the national and regional backbone operators who run the high-speed lines and equipment that form the underlying structure or "backbone" of the Internet. These backbone operators usually connect several major cities with high-speed leased lines and extend those connections to surrounding areas with slower lines.

You can also find jobs with companies that maintain the Network Access Points (NAPs) that provide the basis for interconnectivity between the backbone operators. Originally, there were four NAPs in New York; Washington, D.C.; Chicago; and San Francisco. New ones have been added in San Jose, California, and in the East.

There are also jobs with Internet service providers (ISPs), which include such giants as America Online (www.corp.aol.com), Net-Zero (www.NetZero.net), Microsoft (www.msn.com), and Earth-Link (www.earthlink.net), as well as smaller regional and local providers. Finally, many businesses need to create their own internal networks (intranets) to provide secure business communications within companies as well as a connection to the resources of the Internet.

A National Internet Service Provider

The first online consumer service was America Online (AOL), which was founded in 1985. It also was the first service to provide an instant messaging service, parental controls, and "anywhere" e-mail. Today, AOL has about thirty million subscribers around the world who send roughly 450 million e-mails a day as well as about 1.5 billion instant messages. Plus, AOL has approximately 170,000 chat rooms operating every day. In addition, subscribers have access to an array of exclusive online news, music, video, and sports content. There is also a package of communications and community features, safety and security tools, and on-demand content, video clips, and more than two hundred CD-quality radio stations for AOL's four million broadband subscribers.

Because AOL offers so many services and has so many subscribers, it employs several thousand people. A visit to the AOL website lets you see the wide variety of jobs available for computer buffs in areas from customer support to Web applications to network technical operations.

Training Opportunities. AOL offers an internship program that gives practical real-world experience to prepare young people for future careers. It is a chance to show one's talents to hiring managers with the possibility of working for AOL after graduation. It is a very competitive program with the following minimum requirements. You must be:

- enrolled in school at the time of internship
- eighteen or older at the time of hire
- highly motivated and resourceful with strong academic standing
- available to work a minimum of eight weeks
- eligible to work permanently in the United States

Besides the intern program, AOL has co-op programs that allow students to work part-time or full-time during a semester and receive course credit. This work experience ties directly to their area of study and interests. Students are only hired from colleges that have formal co-op programs run through their career offices. Other ISPs also offer internship and co-op programs. Both are excellent ways to not only learn more about the Internet work world, but also to possibly obtain future employment with an ISP.

A Smaller Internet Service Provider

Not all ISPs are huge companies with millions of subscribers. Many are local and regional companies that generally operate in just a few telephone area codes. Jim Deibele started Teleport in 1987 with one PC in a spare bedroom. It is not as easy now to launch a new Internet service provider as it presently takes a substantial amount of money to buy the equipment to provide the necessary level of service.

Jim's company became the preeminent Internet provider in the Northwest, serving more than twenty thousand subscribers in Oregon and Southwest Washington. The company employed about seventy people in a community-oriented business that offered support and special discounts to teachers, librarians, and nonprofit organizations.

The two largest employee categories at the firm were customer service representative and technical service representative. Other jobs associated with the Web included Web content developer and Web designer. And of course, as in every business, there were jobs in operations, accounting, and human resources.

Teleport also offered virtual server accounts. A virtual server allows individuals or companies to run their personal websites from an ISP's server as if the websites had their own dedicated Internet connection. Before the Internet bubble burst, Teleport was sold to EarthLink.

A Closer Look at ISP Job Opportunities

Technical support is the most labor-intensive position in most ISPs. These people can be called "real bridge people" because of the connection they provide between the ISP and the consumer. This is a transferable skill in that a good tech can go anywhere and find a job.

There is also a continued demand for systems operators who can understand and manipulate the backbone and for creative services personnel who are versed in Web authoring languages. On either company websites or giant online job billboards, you can see thousands of jobs available at ISPs. Here are two sample job descriptions found online:

JUNIOR SALES ACCOUNT EXECUTIVE

Previous Experience: one to three years of business-to-business sales experience

Requirements: Bachelor's degree

Job Description: Sell Internet data. Find and develop new customer relationships with small to medium-sized businesses. Manage the sales process from beginning to end. Respond to and follow up on sales inquiries by telephone, mail, and personal visits.

INFORMATION SYSTEMS TECHNICIAN

Previous Experience: six months to one year of experience supporting PCs and peripherals

Requirements: High school diploma or GED with one to two years of experience as an associate client support technician or equivalent or bachelor's degree with appropriate certification

Job Description: Investigate and resolve reported or assigned PC and telephony-related hardware, software, and feature-related problems and issues. Identify potential end-user difficulties and work with team members to avert or minimize service disruptions. Test and evaluate hardware and software to determine efficiency, reliability, and compatibility with existing systems. Manage daily workload of routine and unscheduled service requests. Support other operations personnel with network troubleshooting issues.

Outfitting Companies and Individuals with the Proper Hardware

The Internet is on a continuous cycle in which each advance in programs and services stimulates a demand for increased speed, and each advance in speed opens up a new area of possible services. The market for people to design and build Internet hardware should be strong for the foreseeable future, although just which line or piece of hardware will be the standard in the future is still to be determined.

Today's network is composed of equipment that is designed to work together regardless of the manufacturer, using the common standard TCP/IP (or Transmission-Control Protocol/Internet Protocol). This is called open architecture and is partly responsible for the proliferation of manufacturers as well as the rapid development of new technologies. When each part of a system will work with everyone else's part, then a new component of a system can be developed and integrated without having to rebuild the entire system. Small start-up firms are able to get their products to a market that is no longer the exclusive province of the major firms.

If you are interested in helping to create the physical part of the Internet, you might work for one of the major equipment vendors, such as Cisco Systems (www.cisco.com) or Nortel Networks (www.nortel.com), or for a line provider, such as SBC Communications (www.sbc.com), or Ameritech (www.ameritech.net).

Developing Software for the Internet

Software developments are in large part responsible for the directions in which the Internet has grown. It has provided the protocols that let many different kinds of computers, ranging from PCs to mainframes, talk to each other. The popular e-mail services owe their existence to the evolution of software programs.

The development of Web browsers has led to the great surge in the popularity of Web surfing by providing a simple way to navigate the Web by clicking on links using the mouse. Three of the major browsers are Netscape's Navigator (www.netscape.com), Microsoft's Internet Explorer (www.microsoft.com), and Foxfire (www.mozilla.com).

Search engines that use the Web browser interface have made it possible for Web users to find the information they seek, whether it is a place to buy a piano or to find out the population of Tokyo. The most popular search engine is Google (www.google.com). Other leading commercial search engines include Yahoo! (www.yahoo.com) and Microsoft (www.msn.com). As a computer buff, you could be the software guru who creates another way for the Internet to grow or who helps companies and individuals use the Net for entertainment or profit.

Helping Companies Get on the Net

As use of the Internet in homes, offices, businesses, the government, and other organizations becomes more and more popular, companies have literally jumped aboard the Net for a variety of reasons. A few companies simply want their stockholders, customers, and employees to think that they are associated with the latest technology, but a great number are using the Net to advertise, market, or sell their products and services. Others want to put information about their companies online to attract investors and customers and to describe employment opportunities.

Whatever the reason, this avalanche of companies that have come aboard the Net means jobs for computer buffs. There are jobs in marketing, advertising, sales, and consulting, as well as jobs in more technical areas such as software engineering and programming. Visit the websites of most large companies, and you'll see many listings for Internet-related jobs.

Webmasters

Once a company has decided to have an Internet presence, it needs someone to build and maintain its website. A successful website is often the result of efforts by a diverse group of people working as a team. The Webmaster is like the captain of a ship or the ringmaster of a circus—in charge of everything. A typical group might include a marketing director, a technical manager, a content manager, a public relations specialist, a graphic artist, and the Webmaster.

The larger the company, the more people there will be working with the Webmaster. It is not unusual to have Web designers, Web technologists, server engineers, software developers, Web administrators, user-interface designers, online documentation managers, creative directors, and Internet engineers, to name just a few positions. Of course, in smaller companies, all of the functions of the Webmaster job are handled by one person.

DUTIES OF A WEBMASTER

- coordinate and evaluate Web development projects
- understand the company's goals
- work with marketing to be sure the website is directed toward the target audience
- have an understanding of design and be able to implement the work of graphic artists
- evaluate and implement Web tools and technology
- monitor Web traffic and determine bandwidth requirements
- maintain and monitor website security

Salary. Pay levels for Webmaster positions vary widely and depend somewhat on the size of the company offering the position as well as on the skill levels and responsibilities required. Salaries for Webmasters average more than $50,000 a year. They range as high as $100,000 or more.

The International Webmaster's Association

The International Webmaster's Association should be the first stop online (www.iwanet.org) for anyone considering a career as a Webmaster. This organization offers articles in its official e-zine on upcoming events and industry news, as well as an experts exchange with more than five thousand experts to help you with difficult questions. In addition, there is a job and resume resource center and a news center. This organization provides more than forty online instructor-led classes and three levels of Webmaster certification.

Providing a Unique Service on the Internet

You don't have to be a technical whiz to work closely with the Internet. One reason the Internet is growing so fast is because it has so many practical uses. The number of unique services that you can find on the Internet continues to expand in many imaginative ways. No longer do people have to visit a bank or brokerage firm; now they can turn their homes into branch banks and buy stocks and bonds using the Internet. Job hunting using the Internet has really taken off and is rapidly changing how professional, managerial, and technical people look for work. Web casting has taken away the need to surf for news, sports, weather, and stock information by delivering the specially tailored information requested by customers directly to their desks. The millions of game players who have become accustomed to playing video games now have the opportunity to play games against or with multiple players on the Internet. Online information services offer access to millions of documents. Students can sit at home or in their dormitories and take college courses online. Plus, you can now buy and sell almost everything under the sun online.

All of these innovations offer a wide range of employment opportunities to match the skills and interests of computer buffs, whether they are technical types who want to work with databases, systems support, or software development, or those who want to be involved with the Internet as customer service representatives, marketing and sales team members, or researchers.

Online Banking—Wells Fargo Bank

More than 150 years ago, Wells Fargo stage coaches traveled across the American West delivering mail and cash. Today the bank is one of the leaders in offering online banking services through the

Internet. Consumers can pay bills, view their account information, transfer money between their Wells Fargo accounts, and receive messages and alerts to stay informed about their accounts. Furthermore, merchants can accept online payments for the goods and services they sell over the Internet with the help of Wells Fargo's secured Internet electronic payment service. Wells Fargo first offered online banking in 1989 and Internet services in 1995.

Wells Fargo has several hundred employees supporting its online business. There are professionals who handle marketing, systems development, channel management, and operational management as well as employees responsible for online customer service. Computer buffs can visit www.wellsfargo.com to view employment opportunities in the Internet Services Division for such positions as product manager, technical support supervisor, senior applications programmer/analyst, website manager, marketing manager, and many others. And, of course, most other banks offer similar online services, making it possible for computer buffs to find jobs just about anywhere in online banking.

Online Job Listing Services

You have so many options for finding out about job openings online. You can go to one of the huge job search engines, such as www.monster.com, www.careerbuilder.com, or http://hotjobs.yahoo.com. Besides being able to search for jobs, you will find advice on resume writing, interviewing, and what salaries to expect in a given field. There will also be information on strategies for job hunting.

In addition, most newspapers have gotten into the online job search game, making their want ad sections available online. Besides this, companies, both large and small, provide employment information on their websites. Each and every one of these websites offers computer buffs jobs from database management to programming to computer technicians to Webmasters to office staff.

When Ken Ramberg graduated from college in 1987, he saw firsthand the inefficiency in the way employers had to post job listings separately to different universities. Along with two partners, he started JobTRAK in 1988 as a central data processing center. Most major university career centers teamed up with JobTRAK to process job listings and make them available to their job seekers via the Web.

Today, JobTRAK, now known as MonsterTRAK, is part of Monster, a giant Internet career company, and can be accessed at www.monstertrak.monster.com. While JobTRAK had only eighty-five employees in 1997, now MonsterTRAK employs several hundred people just on job development.

Selling Products on the Internet

There are abundant opportunities for finding work in online stores. Some only have online sales, while others are the websites for bricks and mortar stores of all sizes, from the giant Wal-Mart to the specialty teddy bear store in the shopping mall. It is getting to be the exception for physical stores not to have a presence on the Web. And all these stores need computer buffs like you to get them online and manage their website operations around the clock. Job opportunities in this area will increase each year because e-commerce is still in its infancy.

If you have an entrepreneurial spirit, you may want to open your own online store. However, there are several reality checks that you need to make. Sales on the Internet are just beginning to boom as individuals become more comfortable with shopping online.

It is not easy to establish a successful online business—knowledge, dedication, and hard work are the key ingredients. Do your homework—learn your way around the Internet and understand your competition before you try to start a business.

Amazon.com—an Amazon-Sized Bookstore

Amazon.com is considered a pioneer, and it has only been doing business since 1995. Today, this online company is the global leader in e-commerce. Amazon.com started out selling books and had more than five times the number of titles that you would find at even the largest land-based chain superstores. Now it offers everything from books and home electronics to tennis rackets and costly diamond jewelry. In 2001, Amazon.com began to offer its e-commerce platform to other retailers and to individual sellers. Big-name retailers work with Amazon Services to power their e-commerce offerings from end to end, including technology services, merchandising, customer service, and order fulfillment. Visit the website at www.amazon.com to see the special features. Then click on "Careers" to discover the many positions available in such areas as programming, customer service, systems administration, Web design, finance, public relations, database architecture, copywriting, and advertising. Here is a description of just one of the many jobs at Amazon.com.

SOFTWARE DEVELOPMENT ENGINEER

We're building cool stuff, we're growing like crazy, and we're having a blast—what more could you ask for? The Order Pipeline Monitoring and Reporting team is seeking sharp, talented, energetic software development engineers to help us meet our ambitious objectives. We are a dynamic, agile team with an awesome mission—we monitor each and every customer order as it moves through Amazon's order fulfillment systems, watch for problems, and drive improvement through the order pipeline. We are the real-time eyes and ears for anyone wanting to know how an order is progressing throughout Amazon.com.

Online Car-Buying Services

Since the majority of car buyers are now surfing the Web before even visiting a dealership and the online purchase of vehicles is increasing, the outlook for a career in this area is steadily growing. For example, car manufacturers have websites with detailed information about their vehicles. There are also independent sites that let you compare the prices and values of both new and used cars, such as www.consumerreports.org, www.edmunds.com, and www .kbb.com. Other websites help consumers actually find or buy a vehicle.

CarSmart went online at www.carsmart.com in the third quarter of 1996 to assist consumers in locating, pricing, and purchasing or leasing new or used vehicles. Business really took off. One year later, the website was receiving twenty thousand requests a day from consumers wanting to find nearby dealers who had specific vehicles. And within one more year, the volume of requests had more than tripled, and the staff required to handle the work had doubled. Today, CarSmart is part of Autobytel, Inc., a leading Internet automotive marketing services company that helps retailers sell cars and manufacturers build brands through marketing, advertising, and data and customer relationship management products and programs. Visit CarSmart at www.carsmart.com to see all of the services that are provided, from quoting the price of new cars and the location of dealers to buying and selling used cars to comparison pricing to information centers for insurance, finance, and warranties.

Online Auction Giant eBay

Founded at the same time as Amazon.com, eBay brought a new concept to the Internet. It started an online website where practically anyone could trade practically anything. Today, more than a hundred million users from around the world are visiting the website to buy and sell thousands of items, from CDs to used cars to toys to jewelry to clothing. Buyers can purchase items in an auction-style format or at a fixed price. It is the most popular shopping destination on the Web, with people from all over the world shopping there. Because of its size, the company needs skilled computer buffs for a wide range of jobs. Here are the job requirements for one position.

> ### STAFF INFORMATION SECURITY ENGINEER
> Personal attributes required:
> - ability to communicate effectively, both verbally and in writing
> - strong sense of professionalism and ethics
> - enthusiasm and interest in information and network security
> - initiative to take on tasks without prompting—a self-starter
> - ability to work as a member of a large security team

Keeping up with Changes on the Internet

For dedicated computer buffs, the Internet is the communications channel of the computer world. Use it to keep yourself informed about what is happening in the computer industry. Use it to chat with computer professionals and to find out about job openings and companies. Visit the home pages of Internet magazines and newspapers frequently to look for career and technology information. Check what is happening at companies like Microsoft and Netscape—leading players in the Internet world. As you become more and more knowledgeable about the Net, bookmark those sites that offer the solid career information you want. And have fun surfing!

CHAPTER TEN

Computer Careers in Jobs from A to Z

Computers have become absolutely essential to the business of running companies, organizations, and the government. Record keeping has largely been handed over to computers, along with so many other jobs. And the workplace has been extended beyond the office to homes, planes, and just about everywhere through the use of computers. It is becoming quite difficult today to find a job that does not involve the use of a computer in some way. Police have them in their patrol cars, pilots use them to fly planes, engineers use them to design roads and bridges, and lawyers research legal issues on them. Indeed, this is the Information Age, with computers in Fortune 500 companies, firehouses, supermarkets, hotels, auto repair shops, restaurants, offices, factory floors, operating rooms, dairy barns, and just about every other workplace imaginable.

Computer-Related Jobs from A to Z

Much to the delight of computer buffs, almost every job in this century is involved in some way with the computer. This chapter explores the use of computers in a wide variety of jobs, from architect to zoo manager.

A Is for Accountant, Actuary—and Architect

Anthony Poon is an award-winning architect. In 2004, he was recognized for designing the most outstanding elementary school in the United States. When he graduated from college in 1986, the first version of computer-aided design (CAD) had just emerged, but architects were still doing most of their work by hand. Even in graduate school at Harvard, no CAD classes were offered. In fact, they wouldn't become mandatory until a few years later. When Anthony entered the workplace, he would sketch or draft by hand, and the hand-drawing was input into the computer so size and scale could easily be changed. This is the way some lead designers like Anthony are still using this technology. Others are doing all their design work on the computer. Today, it is even possible to have three-dimensional drawings. What the computer has done is to speed up the design process, especially with its ability to change such elements as size and scale so rapidly.

At times, Anthony does, however, complete a design from start to finish on the computer. Often, it is a small project, such as the design of a railing for a deck. He is largely self-taught in CAD. The introductory course that he took as an undergraduate in CAD has no relevance to what can be done with CAD today.

In his own architecture firm, the computer is used for far more than design work. It is used for all graphics work, especially the design of flyers and brochures. Plus, it is used for financial records, writing letters, and just about everything else associated with the business of running his firm.

B Is for Banker, Broker—and Beautician

Kenn Williams is a distinguished hairdresser and a computer buff who is very glad the computer age is here. Kenn would not like to run or work in a salon without a computer. Computers help Kenn with the business side of hairdressing in scheduling appointments, doing the payroll, keeping an inventory of all retail sales in the shop, and handling all his bookkeeping chores. The computer is a true time-saver for Kenn. For example, instead of taking six to eight hours to do the payroll every week, the computer lets him finish this task in minutes and even prints out the payroll checks.

But beyond this, the computer is an aid in the artistic side of hairdressing. By just pushing a few keys on the computer keyboard, Kenn can find out the correct hair color for individual clients as well as the date of their last perm. With computer imaging, clients can now know what they will look like with a certain hairstyle and color. In the future, Kenn believes that clients will not have to wait until they arrive at a salon to get this visual image of themselves. It will become customary for clients to contact salons online to tell hairdressers what they want to look like for a special event even before they arrive for their appointments.

C Is for Curator, Composer—and Copyeditor

L. T. Brown is one of several copyeditors at the *Indianapolis News*. Copyeditors review and edit the work of reporters so it is ready to be set in type. At the start of L.T.'s day, thirty or forty stories may be stored in the newspaper's computer system waiting to be edited. Reporters have written the stories and given them to their editors, who may have made some changes. The editors have also placed instructions on the stories detailing what kind of headlines are to be used and what the size of the story should be (column length and width). These stories are then sent to the copy chief—the editor who parcels out assignments and makes sure that the copyeditors are working on what is needed. All this is now done by computer on most newspapers.

L.T. pulls a story up on his computer monitor, and the copyediting process begins. As L.T. reads through the copy, he edits. At times, he must do considerable rewriting to meet space specifications that are sometimes so tight that he may substitute the word *try* for *attempt*, for example. By the press of a button on his computer, L.T. can tell whether the story is the correct length. When the correct length is achieved, L.T. writes the headline and then sends it all to the copy chief, who glances through it for any errors L.T. has not caught and sends it to typesetting. The computer has truly replaced the copyeditor's pencil.

D is for Detective, Designer—and Druggist

Rosie Perez is a druggist at a large chain drugstore. Call in a refill, request one online, or bring a refill prescription in person, and she quickly pulls the prescription up on her computer. Then the computer prints the label, and Rosie fills the prescription. If you have a new prescription, she enters it into the computer, which then prints the label. The first time customers visit her drugstore to fill a prescription, they also complete a form giving information about allergies, health conditions, and prescription insurance plans. Rosie enters all of this information in the computer. If a customer's new prescription conflicts with other medications or is contraindicated because of allergies or health conditions, the computer alerts Rosie to this fact. In addition, the computer prints insurance forms for customers needing them. It also bills insurance companies directly for some customers. Besides serving as a druggist's helper and bookkeeper, the computer also keeps inventory of all the drugs that are sold and updates the inventory on a weekly basis. The inventory list goes by computer to company headquarters so that drugs can be replenished automatically when the weekly supply truck arrives. Rosie considers the computer to be a valuable aid in completing her work.

E is for Editor, Engineer—and Educator

The computer is now part of almost every classroom. It has greatly extended the boundaries of the classroom through Internet access. It has also made teaching and record keeping much easier for teachers. Olivia Jones is one example of a teacher who really takes advantage of the role computers can play in education. As a reading teacher in a middle school, she is able to have each and every one of her students work in the school's computer lab on a reading program that is just right for their skill level at least once a week. Then she has additional computers in her classroom that can be used for more individual and small-group work. Olivia even uses a computer program to create individual lessons for some of her students. The program allows her to add her own voiced comments.

Olivia has not only embraced computers for individual work, she also uses them to present special instruction to the entire class. She uses it to keep grades and has found it is a whiz in figuring average scores on tests. Furthermore, e-mail has given her much closer contact with both parents and students. Because she works at a school whose faculty has truly embraced the use of the computer, her attendance records are computerized and so are the report cards.

F is for Farmer, Food Inspector—and Firefighter

David L. Klingler is the chief inspector of a fire prevention division. When he began working at the fire station in 1986, all files were manual and all reports were typewritten. David, who used his home computer for playing games, began taking the schedules home to put on his computer. The chief was so impressed with David's work that he purchased a computer for the firehouse. David admits to making every mistake in the book before learning how to use the computer, but he ultimately succeeded in giving the computer a vital role at his fire station.

Today, the fire alarm system is completely automated. The computer now gives the station ready access to information about all the buildings in the district. By pushing a few keys, David or any of the other firefighters can find out the size of the building, the type of alarm system that the building has, and who occupies the building. The location of fire extinguishers also is stored on the computer as well as when they were last serviced. Furthermore, all the fire inspectors now carry handheld computers instead of clipboards to inspection sites. They punch in record numbers and codes along with a 144-letter description to complete inspections. When the inspectors return to the station, the information can be uploaded quickly into the station's computer, and in less than one minute a printout of the inspection is available. The computer also has helped the firefighters cut 95 percent of all the writing involved in keeping track of hoses and hydrants. In addition, the station can get information and reports on fire responses and fatalities by linking its computer to one in Washington, D.C. The computer has truly become a firefighter at David's station.

G is for Geologist, Graphic Artist—and General Manager

Mark Goff studied music and business in school and is now the general manager of a music store. At his store, the employees cannot do their jobs without using the computer, as everything they do is linked to it. All sales transactions and product information is entered into the computer. Records of the store's inventory and sales are kept on the computer. Customer correspondence and intra-office memorandums are done on the computer. The computer is even used to produce the company's bar codes.

Here's an example of how the store uses its computer system: Mark just purchased two trombones. They were immediately entered into the computer as a purchase. Then bar code labels were printed to identify the instruments. The repair shop input the work history of each instrument. This allows the music store to update an instrument's condition in the computer if it were to return to the store for resale or repair.

Another task the computer has assumed is keeping track of the musical instruments the music store leases to over one hundred schools in the state. This involves billing over one thousand customers every month—a formidable job without the computer. Even though his store is completely computerized, Mark's background only includes one computer course, which was programming. He points out that most of the computer programs the store uses are very user friendly. Because the menu program is so good, most staff members can usually figure out at once how to use the computer for their tasks.

H is for Historian, Hotel Staffer—and Horse Farm Owner

At Glenmore Farm in Lexington, Kentucky, the owners Barbara, Clay, and Jeff Camp are using computers to help them run their 285-acre horse farm. An amazing amount of information has been stored on the computer for each of the approximately 175 horses on the farm at any one time. With this information, the Camps are able to know the exact location on the farm of each horse and what kind of horse it is, from a yearling to a racehorse. The computer also is used to keep track of breeding dates and when horses should foal. If anyone on the farm needs to know the health history of a horse, when a horse needs a blacksmith, or when a horse will come in season, the answer is stored in the computer. Information about the arrival and departure of horses also can be found in the computer. Some mares from other states only visit the farm seasonally for breeding purposes. Information about what van company will be transporting a horse and what necessary health papers must go with it also can be found in the computer files.

When farm manager Jeff Camp goes on his daily visit to the barn, he does not bring pencil and paper but a laptop computer to note any actions he has taken with the horses. At the end of his daily rounds, he takes the laptop back to the office and uploads the data he has entered into the computer's master files.

The computer operates throughout the day at Glenmore Farm. All the billing and check writing for bills and payroll are done on the computer. Besides instantly providing information about the horses, the computer saves the farm money. When it is time to take the year's records to the accountant, everything is already itemized. Barbara believes that if the computer were not helping them run the farm, they would need to hire additional people. She also finds the computer invaluable in researching a horse's background. By using a computer data bank such as Jockey Club, she can check a horse's parentage, age, track earnings, and sales results. She can even register a horse by using the computer modem.

I is for Instructor, Investigator—and Indexer

An index is the alphabetical list of names and subjects together with the page numbers that tell where they appear in the text of a book. Indexers compile these lists, which are typically found in the back of books. Claire Bolton feels very lucky to have the computer help her with her work as an indexer. There are special programs that she uses to do this work. The computer has freed her from worrying so much about clerical details and allowed her to concentrate on the quality of what she is producing. The advent of the computer has cut the number of indexers required on the staffs of book companies. Many indexers, like Claire, are freelancers.

J is for Judge, Jeweler—and Jailer

Norman Bucker is assistant jail commander of a large metropolitan jail that houses fifteen hundred inmates. The computer system is up and running every day. It is a fantastic management tool that lets Norman and others on the jail staff know myriad details about the prisoners just by pressing a few buttons. The computer has information on where prisoners are located, movement of prisoners, rule violations prisoners have committed, past stays in prison, prison escapes, and what type of prisoner an individual is. Information is so detailed that the staff is able to find every car that is registered to a prisoner's family.

At this large jail, everything is done on the computer, from visitations to library visits for inmates to employee attendance records. The computer system makes it possible to send memos and contact individuals such as prosecutors without having to spend hours playing phone tag. Jail policy can be created, adjusted, or even changed without too much difficulty. Using the computer has helped the jail staff cut down on paperwork, is cost effective, and has improved the overall management of the jail.

K is for Kindergarten Teacher—and Kennel Owner

Rick Smith is the owner of two kennels in Michigan. He realized that customers often made plans for the care of their pets over the phone and then changed their instructions when the pets were left at the kennel. In order to keep the pet owners happy and to provide the proper care for their pets, Rick developed several kennel software programs.

The programs are now being used by kennels throughout the country. Rick points out that so much of the successful operation of a kennel involves communication, and the computer helps to eliminate problems by storing information in such a way that everyone has access to it. For example, kennel caregivers need to know the proper diet for each animal, and the computer stops workers from misreading another person's abbreviations or scribbles. The computer prints out a card that is put on each pet's run. The card tells the animal's name, breed, weight, color, and diet and lists any toys or other items that the animal has brought to the kennel. (Rick has had animals come with their own monogrammed Gucci luggage.) By looking at the computer-printed card, an employee quickly can see what care an animal requires and if the right animal is in a run.

The computer has been so helpful to Rick that he is able to run his Michigan kennels in the winter from his home in Florida. Every day, Rick can find out how many different animals entered and left his kennels and the number of animals that were groomed. He is able to determine what the day's income was as well as check on the inventory at each kennel. The computer has enabled Rick to arrange his business so he can have other people actually see to the day-to-day operations.

Rick sees the computer as the catalyst for the development of chains of kennels. He believes that pet owners will get better care for their animals in these major operations because of the availability of professional advice on diet and animal health.

Shawn Robertson, a manager at a kennel using KennelSoft soft-ware, says the computer is the heart of their business. Shawn explains that every time a dog is checked in or out of the kennel, it is entered in the computer database. In addition, special nota-tions on personality problems can be stored in the computer. Shawn adds that the computer also does inventory, keeping track of everything in the retail area. In addition, the computer is used to determine how many animals can be accommodated at the kennel. This is especially important during the busy holiday peri-ods, when so many different animals are vying for a limited num-ber of spaces.

L is for Loan Officer, Legal Secretary—and Librarian

Suzanne Braun has been the librarian at the Indianapolis Zoo for several years. Suzanne, who has a master's degree in library sci-ence, points out that computer classes are mandatory for librar-ians as the computer has become such an important tool in libraries. Like that of all librarians, much of her workday involves using the computer.

The Indianapolis Zoo is part of the Indiana Department of Education's computer access network (IDEANET), which ties together schools and businesses in the state of Indiana to provide information to students and teachers. Using this computer system, Suzanne spent one hour recently with a third grade class. During this live computer chat, students took turns typing in their ques-tions about animals and received immediate input from Suzanne on their computer. She also spends many hours a day doing research on the computer system that links all public, academic, and special libraries across the country. This system enables her to track down books and articles through interlibrary loan and have a copy of the book or article sent to her. Suzanne is also one of a group of zoo and aquarium librarians in the United States who share information. For example, when she creates a bibliography on a certain animal, the information can be uploaded into another zoo librarian's system in another part of the country.

Suzanne spends additional time on the computer going through her e-mail messages and sending replies back to teachers and students wanting zoo-related information. She also uses e-mail to communicate with other zoo librarians. She sorts through her e-mail and keeps the information that will be helpful to zoo staff members.

M is for Mathematician, Mechanic—and Music Copyist

Music copyists transcribe each individual musical part from a score onto paper. For example, a copyist will go through a complete score and write out the entire part for the violin, making it much easier for the violinist to play his or her part. In the past, copying was done by hand with a special pen. Today, however, copyists can play on a keyboard directly into a computer. The information is then translated into printed notations.

Jeff Wiedenfeld and his wife, Julie, run Blue Note Engraving, a company that copies music. Their company is fully computerized, and the speed of the computer is very important in getting music to the clients on time. According to Jeff, the computer does it all. Publishing houses, music groups, and composers need copies quickly, and with the computer he can get copy to a publisher— even one in London—without much delay. Julie and Jeff do no copying by hand because they have instructed the computer to do it all. Although their business is based in the Midwest, they have clients throughout the world.

N is for Nurse, Nutritionist—and Newspaper Manager

Karen Braeckel is the manager of the educational services department of a major metropolitan newspaper. Her job is to encourage the reading of newspapers in the classroom. The Newspaper in

Education program develops educational materials for teachers to use with students and gives workshops on using the newspaper in the classroom. Most of the work is done on the community relations department's four computers. Karen writes articles and memos on the computer to pass on to other newspaper employees. When one of the articles is ready to be printed in the newspaper, Karen sends it directly to the composing room. Karen is a true computer buff who says she could not possibly produce what she does today if she did not have access to a computer.

Karen Sprunger also works in educational services. She learned how to use the computer by simple trial and error. In her present job, Karen uses the computer for a variety of tasks, including writing letters, editing or compiling materials for teachers, designing student worksheets, formatting reports for committees, and creating special calendars and materials. What she likes best about the computer is the freedom it gives her to move text. Karen spends her workdays creating pages exactly the way she wants them to look. Karen enjoys using the computer in her job and is happy that she no longer has to spend as much time cutting and pasting layouts.

O is for Optometrist—and Officer in the Army

Dana Ball was issued a computer before her freshman year began at West Point, and when she graduated she took the computer with her to her first assignment. At West Point the computers were interfaced with Kermit—a network mail system that allowed cadets to log on to the system and communicate both with other cadets in the corps and with professors. Dana used the computer for all her classes, from English to calculus. She also spent five to eight hours a day on it in her senior year, as she had selected the systems engineering track as her engineering area, and all work was done on the computer.

As a second lieutenant and the executive officer for a two- to four-hundred-soldier advanced individual training company,

Dana's main assignment was to relieve the administrative burden of her commander. She planned the training of the soldiers and used the computer to create hard copy of the training schedule. In order to accomplish this mission, she spent time creating short-, medium-, and long-range calendars on the computer. Without the computer, it would have taken Dana countless hours to produce her weekly training schedules. By using the computer she was able to bring up previous schedules and keep all the items that remain the same each week, such as wake-up and bed-check times. The computer was also an invaluable tool in handling her other duties. Dana used the Harvard Graphics program to print awards for the soldiers. And she used the computer to handle the paperwork for her other duties, which include serving as the local unit drug and alcohol testing officer, the moral welfare and recreation officer, and a member of the officer's club and the arts and crafts councils.

P is for Postal Clerk, Paralegal—and Pilot

Doug Allington is a senior pilot flying an MD-80 for Northwest Airlines. Almost everything he does as a pilot is related in some way to computers. When he bids for routes each month, the computer assigns him and the other pilots to routes by seniority. Upon arriving at the airport for a flight, a clerk punches his employee number into a computer, and the computer gives him a list of the flight crew. Then an hour before takeoff, he receives a computer printout from the flight planning computer listing such things as weather at takeoff, weather at destination, in-route weather, time of trip, routing, winds at cruise altitude, and fuel load. The computer also predicts the plane weight, winds, and temperature at takeoff and gives the optimal runway and takeoff speed. Just before the door closes, the computer provides him with the final weight. Once the plane is on the runway, Doug takes over and the computer doesn't have much to do. Of course, the computers in the control tower are busy tracking all the planes. A computer aboard the MD-80, which is taking in information from all over the plane, can land the plane in really bad weather. Doug puts information about the heading, course, and speed in this computer. A computer used in aircraft communications addressing and reporting sends information about arrival and departure times and delays to the airline computer system. This updates the arrival time you see on the screens at the airport. Doug also can use this computer to send in maintenance reports.

According to Doug, the MD-80 has only a first-generation computer system, while the airline's airbuses are the most computerized commercial planes. On the airbuses, the pilot watches six monitors instead of gauges, the plane is steered by a joystick instead of a wheel, and the computer monitors the pilot's actions and will not let pilots exceed the performance limit of the plane. The pilots who fly these planes are acting like computer systems managers. Doug says that today's pilots must be computer wise because computers play such an important role in all aspects of flying.

Q is for Quilter—and Quality-Control Technician

Engineers design the printers manufactured by the Silicon Valley company where Mary Lai works as a quality-control technician. Her job is to make sure the production model meets the engineers' design standards. Before the advent of computerized testing, most quality-control work was done by selecting a sample of the factory's products and then measuring or testing the product to see if it worked as it was designed to. In some cases, this actually involved tearing products apart to see that they were made correctly. Using this approach meant that not every product could be tested.

In Mary's company every printer is tested to ensure it meets the design parameters. This is possible because the company uses a computer-based system with special sensors that quickly tell if the printer is meeting acceptable limits. The computer is actually making 100 percent quality control possible.

R is for Realtor, Reporter—and Reservation Clerk

Carol Love is a reservation sales representative for an international airline. During her eight-and-one-half-hour workday, she spends approximately seven hours and forty minutes in front of a computer handling requests for reservations. She also can change or cancel reservations simply by modifying the record on the computer. Carol has to be knowledgeable about her company's policies and procedures as well as be aware of special promotions. When Carol first went to work for the airline, all her work was done by slides. Computers were introduced in 1969 and since then have been upgraded frequently to more efficient models that have much less downtime. Even though the computer makes Carol's job much easier, she still finds herself, at times, suffering from eyestrain at the end of her shift, even with special screens designed to reduce glare.

S is for Secretary, Sheriff—and Systems Accountant

Les Gisler works on a computer four or five hours a day as a systems accountant. He uses his terminal to interact with the mainframe to extract financial reports for end users who are usually staff accountants. He also uses the computer to solve accounting problems and improve the handling of information. Away from the computer, he trains accountant technicians in the use of hardware as well as the programs that he has designed. Les also has the task of coordinating major system changes between the programming staff and the accounting function.

The position of systems accountant requires a solid background in both computer science and accounting. Les was introduced to computers in the early 1970s, when he was in the army and took a data systems course that covered programming and included an introduction to hardware and systems analysis. After he left the service, Les completed his degree in accounting. Several years later, his growing interest in the data processing side of accounting compelled him to return to school to earn an associate's degree in computer technology. This additional degree helped him obtain his present position as a systems accountant.

T is for Therapist, Ticket Seller—and Tennis Coach

P. A. Nilhagen is a tennis coach of professional and college players as well as junior players. During a match, a tennis expert can key into a computer what is happening on the court. The computer can then produce charts giving coaches and players a statistical breakdown on such things as percentage of good first serves, the effectiveness of a player's serve in the deuce versus advantage court, a player's rate of success in going to the net, and the number of unforced errors committed. P.A. used the computer with former ATP tour player Todd Witsken and with several professional and college players. He finds that the computer-generated information about a match provides significant help, especially when he is unable to attend a player's match.

P.A. also has discovered that most players are not pleased to read the printout of their matches and see the specific classification of their errors. According to P.A., what the computer cannot produce is a chart of the player's mental state during the match, which is critical in understanding when and why players make errors.

The computer is not just used in tennis to chart play during matches. P.A. considers it a very helpful tool in making draws for tournaments. For example, if a tournament is being held with a draw of sixty-four players, the draw would take hours to make on paper. With the computer, the time can be reduced to eight seconds, once the necessary information has been keyed in. P.A. also finds using the computer at tournament check-in desks to be very helpful, especially in determining whether players have current USTA (United States Tennis Association) numbers.

U is for Underwriter, Urban Planner—and Undergraduate

Before most college students enter the job market, they have started working with computers. Besides having science laboratories, colleges now have computer laboratories. And many colleges have elaborate networks that connect to every living group or even every student's room. Aaron Ball is a senior at a private university with a double major in Spanish and political science. Similar to most undergraduates, he took a computer class in high school and has taken two classes in college. Aaron has his own computer at college, and he also uses the computers on campus. He believes that word processing is critical to his academic success, since college professors expect all assignments to be word processed. He keeps all his work on the computer so that revisions can be made easily. And he also uses the computer in managing his time as he keeps a running file on his current projects. In addition, as president of the university's Political Science Association, he uses graphics programs extensively to print schedules and announcements of upcoming events and speakers. After graduation Aaron plans to enter law school, and his computer will be going right along with him.

V is for Veterinarian—and Volunteer

Volunteering has always been a part of the American culture and one of its greatest resources. In recent years the number of volunteers has swelled, and many of these volunteers are computer buffs who use the computer in their volunteer work. Steve Johnson has worked as a volunteer for the American Red Cross for several years.

Because all the organization's computers are linked together, data can be sent quickly and easily to its regional headquarters. The Red Cross also uses its computers to generate postcards reminding blood donors and others of appointments. With increased use of the computer, volunteers like Steve are able to help the Red Cross operate more efficiently as well as have more time for humanitarian efforts in place of paperwork.

W is for Writer, Ward Attendant—and Weather Forecaster

In 1982, Chuck Lofton became a full-time weather forecaster for a national television network and started spending most of his workday on the computer. He creates his own graphics for his weather segments on television; however, he also can obtain computer-generated graphics. Chuck accesses all his weather information via the computer from the national weather station. He can even get an update on the weather immediately before he goes on the air.

Chuck believes that advances in technology will bring higher resolution and cleaner pictures, more animation, and better presentations of the weather on television. New technology will bring him even more information, especially in tracking severe weather. Using a computer is an absolute necessity for weather forecasters as it helps them forecast the weather more accurately.

X is for X-Ray Technologist

Constance Murray works in the x-ray department of a major metropolitan hospital. She points out that the application of computer technology has absolutely revolutionized the field of radiology. Computed tomographic (CT) scanning has employed computers since its inception. In CT scanning, three-dimensional reconstruction of two-dimensional images is possible with computers. These three-dimensional anatomic images can be rotated to visualize the structure in any plane. Orbital fractures and many facial reconstructive surgeries utilize these capabilities. Computer technology also is employed in digital radiography and fluoroscopy, which are becoming routine procedures in the clinical setting. Magnetic resonance imaging (MRI) also applies computer technology similar to CT. With MRI, images of patient anatomy are stored in the computer as bits of data, which can then be printed on film for hard copy and storage retrieval. Anatomical images digitized on a computer also allow manipulation of the image to highlight pathology or better demonstrate organs not otherwise seen well. According to Constance, the advances the computer has brought to radiology make her believe that *Star Trek*–quality medical care is not far away.

Y is for YMCA Employee

William Graham works as vice president/controller at the YMCA headquarters in a Midwestern city. The main computer is at headquarters and is linked to computers at the other YMCAs in the eight-county area. There also are several PCs in the headquarters office and in branches that help with maintaining correspondence, creating brochures, and monitoring program attendance. William says that the computer really helps him to do his job, as nonprofit organizations have to collect so much data for reports to the United Way and various units of government. The computer is used to keep track of revenues for the monthly reports and all financial work in the accounting and payroll departments. It also is used to keep track of all the members and the programs in which they participate.

Other YMCA employees are also turning to computers to help them do their jobs. Debi Roy works as director of aquatics at a small YMCA in Illinois. The computer allows Debi to keep organized records of all the swim classes, teachers, and students. She has also put together a staff member database that lists the certifications and work experience of each of her staff members. This allows her to find vital information quickly. Being able to store all this information in a computer, rather than in filing cabinets, has made Debi's desk area a lot cleaner.

Z is for Zoologist—and Zoo Manager

F. Kevin Gaza works in the business management office of the zoo. He says that the computer helps the zoo in business applications, animal management, and animal record keeping. ARKS is the database system used in keeping a detailed history of all animals. This is very important as it helps to avoid the interbreeding of vanishing wildlife. For example, there are not a lot of Siberian tigers in captivity, so finding a mate is not easy. However, by using the ARKS database, the zookeeper can find every Siberian tiger in captivity and know what its gene makeup is. ISIS (International Species Information System) keeps such detailed information on its database that the exact breeding time of any animal can be swiftly ascertained for stud purposes. Zoo managers also use the Web to obtain information on animals. There are now more than one thousand sites available for this purpose. Some sites feature experts who can be contacted for more detailed questions.

CHAPTER ELEVEN

Computer Careers in the Future

E xciting new technology is developed every day in the computer industry. The future is very promising for computer buffs just beginning their careers and for those already in a computer career. The United States continues to be a world leader in the Information Age, a world in which there is a robust demand for workers who are highly skilled in the use of information technology. Although the explosive growth of the computer industry that began in the 1990s has slowed down due to its large size, it is still growing faster than most large industries. Some areas within the industry will explode and grow at absolutely fantastic rates in the future.

Future Trends

The U.S. Bureau of Labor Statistics recently listed the fastest-growing, highest-paying occupations through 2012. Of the top ten careers listed, eight are computer-related:

- network systems analysts
- database administrators
- computer support specialists
- computer software engineers for applications and systems
- network and computer systems administrators
- computer system analysts
- desktop publishers

What the next hot job areas will be depends on emerging technology and applications. Computer buffs who stay abreast of what is happening in the industry will find exciting career opportunities. For example, "mobile technology," which includes wireless Internet, or WiFi, is rapidly evolving. The expansion of this technology over the next ten years will result in the need for mobility consultants who can help individuals and companies develop and implement systems that can be used on wireless networks.

Here are some of the job areas that computer buffs may wish to explore in the future as many industry experts see promising career opportunities in these areas.

Communications

Millions of cellular telephones are used every day throughout the United States and the world. Cell phones are becoming more sophisticated, with many features that keep users connected. In the near future, cell phones will be able to take high-resolution, multimegapixel photos; stream TV and feature-length videos; and play games with realistic 3-D imaging. This will be possible with cell phones equipped with hard drives—some with capacities as high as ten gigabytes. Developers are even working on cell phones that can switch between digital cellular networks and decide which network has the lowest price for service.

Wireless networking for home and business computers is growing rapidly. Development of WiFi hotspots has kept people connected when they are away from home. Cities like New York, Chicago, San Francisco, and Seattle have hundreds of WiFi hotspots. Computer buffs will find opportunities with companies that are expanding WiFi into areas not already serviced. The next generation of wireless networking is already under way. WiMax, which provides a network signal for up to thirty miles, is in its infancy. Engineers are and will be needed for the development and implementation of this new technology.

Security

Almost all large companies and many small businesses are using local-area networks (LANs). Many of these same companies have Internet websites through which they conduct business. Securing these networks has become a huge concern. It seems a daily occurrence to learn about companies whose computer network servers have been hacked into. In addition, computer viruses are becoming more complex, and it is getting harder to remove them from a system. Programmers, engineers, and systems managers will be needed to develop antivirus software and hardware to keep hackers out and prevent security attacks. Keeping customer data secure will continue to be a major priority for companies as they conduct more and more of their business on the Internet.

Systems Integration

Organizations want to integrate different hardware, operating systems, and applications software so that they can share information with each other. As so many organizations have this need, both in-house staff and outside consultants are needed as system integrators.

Hardware

The working speed of computers has increased enormously since the first personal computer was marketed in the mid 1970s. Some researchers and engineers say the silicon microchip, which most personal computers are based on, has reached it capacity for speed, and that transistors for the processors cannot be made any smaller. Work is being done to create new computer processors that work on the atomic level, where transistors are the size of a single atom. Integrating this new technology into the manufacturing process will be the next challenge for researchers and developers. Carbon nanotubes, nanowires, and spintronics are areas of research to make computer processors faster and more powerful.

Embedded and Invisible Technology

There is a trend in the technology world to make computers vanish from view. Experts are developing ways to embed technology into objects we use every day. Cars already have many computers built into them that control or monitor fuel consumption, brakes, steering, and suspension. The anti-lock braking system (ABS) is a great example of embedded technology. When the driver touches the car's brakes, a computer automatically monitors the system to be sure it stops without the brakes locking and sending the vehicle into a skid. It is not hard to imagine a car that can drive itself. Embedded technology would steer the car by sensing other vehicles and nearby objects. Some car manufacturers are working on a cruise-control system that works with radar systems that have intelligent controls. The controls would automatically respond to other drivers and maintain a safe driving distance between vehicles. These smart cars could conceivably be on autopilot and prevent accidents and save lives. Will you be the computer buff who perfects this concept and makes it available to everyone?

Software

As new hardware is developed, new software is also needed. The tremendous impact of computers and information technology on our everyday lives has created a need to design and develop new computer software systems and to integrate new technologies in a quickly expanding range of applications. Software engineers will find many promising opportunities in the future.

An area of great interest for software and hardware developers is speech recognition. Reliable voice recognition should be common by 2010. In the meantime, the hardware and software has to become more sophisticated to improve accuracy and reduce the error rate of speech recognition in order to better match human capabilities. The challenge of speech recognition is that it requires a human style commonsense reasoning. This is very difficult because decision making is more complex than a mathematical equation. Getting a computer to understand what you say to it and then to behave intelligently is a challenge that will ultimately be solved by a creative computer buff.

Internet

Today the Internet is a big deal. In the future it will be even bigger. The Internet has become irrevocably a part of our everyday life. As more and more people and businesses use the Internet, it has become clogged with e-mail traffic and graphically dense pages, which has caused much of the available bandwidth to be used. The need has arisen for a new Internet. Internet2 (I2) is a consortium of two hundred universities, seventy companies, and forty affiliate organizations—including local, state, and federal government agencies—working together to develop and implement advanced network applications and technologies. The network is expected to provide a consistent 1 gigabit per second transfer rate, about a thousand times faster than today's Internet. Scientists with I2 in September 2004 transferred data on their network at a rate of 6.6 gigabits per second. A transfer rate of 10 gigabits per second is expected very soon. This very high speed network is currently only available to consortium members and is focused on academic needs. But it is expected to develop technology and applications that will eventually be available to everyone.

Computer Careers in Other Job Areas

In the future, computer buffs can look forward to finding computers practically everywhere. No matter where you seek a job, a computer is likely to be involved in some way in your performance of that job. Your home life also will be greatly changed by what your home computer can do for you. Technological innovations in the use of computers have only begun to scratch the surface of their potential. Some researchers believe that the advances will be so great that it is very difficult to make predictions of how the computer will be used just twenty years from now.

Preparing for Your Future Career

Read as much as you can about the computer industry and go aboard the Internet often to find out where the jobs are and what the latest technology is. Explore the field by working part-time and in the summer or by participating in an internship or a cooperative education program. Employers value practical work experience. If you will be getting a degree in computer science, you can be certain the program is a quality one if it is certified by the Accreditation Board for Engineering and Technology (ABET). You can find a list of these schools at www.abet.org.

Remember, too, that computer buffs can find satisfying careers in government, business, education, manufacturing, and anywhere computers are being used. If you are going into business, be sure to get a well-rounded education. According to Max Messmer, chairman of Accountemps, while specialized skills are in growing demand in today's workplace, a general awareness of a broad range of disciplines will allow workers to better apply those skills within a company.